CAROL VORDERMAN'S
DETOX
RECIPES

WITH ANITA BEAN

CHECK WITH YOUR DOCTOR

Before starting this or any other detox diet programme, you should consult your doctor. In particular this should be done with regard to any allergies you have to any of the foods, drinks, products, supplements or other recommendations contained in this programme. The detox diet may not be suitable for everyone. Pregnant women should be especially careful and ensure that their doctor advises that the detox diet is suitable for them. If you are taking medication or have any medical condition, you should check with your doctor first.

While the authors have made every effort to ensure that the information contained in this book is as accurate and up to date as possible, it is advisory only and should not be used as an alternative to seeking specialist medical advice. The authors and publishers cannot be held responsible for actions that may be taken by a reader as a result of reliance on the information contained in this book, which are taken entirely at the reader's own risk.

Dedication

To everyone who worked on this book.
And to the thousands of people who followed the detox and let me know how much it has changed their lives.

Carol Vorderman

Carol Vorderman
Sole Worldwide Representation
John Miles Organisation
Fax: 01275 810186
Email: john@johnmiles.org.uk

Carol Vorderman was assisted in the writing of this book by **Anita Bean** BSc R.PH Nutr., an award-winning nutritionist, magazine columnist and author of twelve top-selling books on food and nutrition.

This edition published in Great Britain in 2005 by
Virgin Books
Thames Wharf Studios
Rainville Road
London W6 9HA

First published in 2003
Copyright © Carol Vorderman 2003, 2005

The right of Carol Vorderman and Anita Bean to be identified as the authors of this work has been asserted by them in accordance with the Copyright, Designs and Patents Act 1988.

A catalogue record for the book is available from the British Library.

ISBN 0 7535 0871 0

All photography by David Loftus
Designed by Smith & Gilmour
Printed and bound in Great Britain by The Bath Press, CPI Group

CONTENTS

CHAPTER 1
INTRODUCTION

Both Detox for Life and the Summer Mini Detox have been bestselling books. Hundreds of thousands of people have tried the detox way of eating and loved it. Some have lost a lot of weight, others now feel much healthier, many have found their skin has improved, their eyes sparkle and the cursed cellulite starts to disappear.

There is no doubt that the detox works and thanks to all of you who've written in. I've had thousands of letters from men and women, some with amazing stories of how they've stuck with the detox for a few months and lost stones in weight. Other times, one person at work has suddenly started to slim down and glow, and inspired by this, the rest of the gang has decided to go on the detox together. There are many stories of entire offices sharing recipes and working a rota of cooking and bringing in lunch for each other. They've had a great time and found it easier when everyone has followed it together. Fantastic.

Others, who have previously had health problems, have found their doctors are astonished at the improvement in their blood cholesterol, and love the fact that they feel healthier than they ever have before.

I've particularly enjoyed being stopped in the street and told personal stories of how detoxers are coping. It's quite funny to be followed round a supermarket to be asked if 'this' or 'that' kind of food is allowed. Mind you, there is a downside. I've been out for dinner and just as I've started munching a plate of Italian grub, a detoxer in the restaurant wanders up and wants to know why I'm not feeling guilty!!! Try and get out of that when you've a shovel full of tiramisu almost at your lips. Not easy. But as you

know, the detox isn't something that stops working when you eat a morsel of non-recommended food. As long as you follow the 80/20 rule everything is fine. That means that when you are 'on the detox' as long as you stick to it for at least 80 per cent of the food you eat, then you will get results. When you're maintaining for the rest of the year, that rule changes yet again and that's why in this Detox Recipes book, we've included menus for the 'strict detox' and for 'maintenance'.

Most detoxers follow one lengthy period (maybe three or four weeks) of detoxing and one shorter period (one or two weeks) every year. In between times we eat well, but not strictly. If you've already 'done a detox', then you'll know that your taste buds change for ever. Somehow, after a detox, you really don't fancy the creamy sauce or the chocolate pudding anymore. If you do choose something really rich, then you can only stomach a small portion, which is fine. I really love fish, so I'll eat fish most days, except when I'm on the detox. I can't eat much red meat and I don't want to. I could barely start, let alone finish, a steak nowadays and I'll often choose the vegetarian option on a menu because it tastes nicer. The great thing is I know that I'm getting all the goodness my body needs.

Being of a certain age (44, although I swear my mother lied about my birthday!), I'm more conscious than ever of the need to be healthy. I've recently had an all-over health check and had the thumbs up for everything (and for that I am truly thankful). It was quite a revelation filling in the form and having to think about 'how many times a week do you eat red meat?' 'how many times do you eat chocolate or sweets?' 'how much bread do you eat every day?' and so on. I hadn't thought about it properly for a long time and I found that the answers were interesting (I even got a smile out of the doctor).

It confirmed that the detox programme (and how it changes what I want to eat) has become part of my life. Probably like you, I've tried dozens of different 'diets' but inevitably, even if I managed to lose some weight, the pounds piled back on the moment I stopped. And that was because they often meant eating processed milkshake 'foods', or bizarre mixtures of foods, or only cabbage soup. One in particular recommends an all protein diet to put your body into an unnatural state of ketosis. This diet seems to be about weight control alone. I don't believe that any diet that says 'eating fruit and veg is bad' can be good for you in the long term. What none of these diets do is to educate you to want to eat the right foods. The detox has done that for hundreds of thousands of people. I've found it's now easy to keep the weight off and the health kick going. Having said that, there have been times over the last five years when life has become too stressful and busy and I've completely caved in for about a month. It's amazing how quickly that sluggish feeling returned and how, when I've consciously changed back to eating well, the energy levels come back.

As every year goes by since I was first introduced to the detox, I'm more convinced than ever that this is the best way to eat for a lifetime's health. And it is the lifetime, not the short term, which matters most.

So when I've looked back at all the emails and letters you've sent in, one of the questions raised most often has been about recipes for when you're not following the strict detox, so that you can maintain healthy eating for ever. 'More recipes, please?' cropped up time and time again. You want more for the strict detox and you want many more for maintenance too. And I'm not surprised: I understand how tricky it can be. When I did my first ever detox, I think I survived on three recipes. Porridge, baked potatoes and squash with salad and non-wheat pasta with a tomato-based sauce. It got a bit boring after a while, which is why when we wrote Detox for Life we included quite a

few recipes. That helped and so did the recipes in the Summer Mini Detox book, and now we've put together an all-new recipe book with sections for all times of the day and all moods.

The recipes marked D are for those who are on the strict detox: and the recipes marked M are for those who are maintaining. Of course, if you are maintaining, then you can choose any recipe. I'm really pleased with the whole selection we've put together – the food tastes fantastic and I've no doubt the recipes will give you lots of pleasure.

Carol Vorderman

P.S. If you've any comments or stories about how the detox has worked for you then please let me know. Write to me at John Miles Organisation, fax: 01275 810186, or email me at john@johnmiles.org.uk or go to www.carolvorderman.net or www.carol-vorderman.com. These websites contain all sorts of extra information plus the chance to take part in future trials.

CHAPTER 2
REAL SUCCESS

Ben Swoyer, 44, finance manager

'For a long time I wanted to lose weight. Despite exercising regularly, my weight had steadily crept up to an unbelievable 16 stone due to my passion for cheese, beer, steaks, barbecued pork and Mexican food. I have always been considered a big eater, something of manly pride. I knew that I needed to change my eating habits to stop me ballooning, but had no clear idea what eating healthily was all about. That is until I went on the detox diet.

My wife bought a copy of Detox for Life and we both started following the diet in January 2003. Beginning the diet was not easy as it took me about two hours to find all the right foods at the supermarket! But now I find shopping really easy. I quickly learned how to drink more water and make delicious smoothies. I have to admit that I did not give up wine completely and sometimes allowed myself the odd pint or two of beer.

I lost about 12lb during the first 28 days and then decided to do it for a further 28 days. I have now lost 20lb, and I feel so much better. I'm fitter and am running faster than ever before. I also enjoy cooking now. I feel like my senses have improved, particularly smell and taste. I sleep better and my allergies seem to have gone. Our kitchen looks fantastic, full of fresh fruits and vegetables. I have also cut down on salt, and I really don't miss meat as much as I thought. That's a big statement from someone who lived in Texas for four years!

The detox diet has changed me for good – I look better, feel better and now have a new appreciation for eating better. Thank you for your diet and a new way of life!'

Lynne Bradley, 57, housewife with three children and one grandchild

'I have arthritis in the top joints of my fingers, which had been very painful, and so I wanted to see whether changing my diet would help. The effect was dramatic. After following the detox diet, I lost nearly a stone, felt great and the pain disappeared from my hands. Apart from the odd twinge, the pain has not returned.

As a keen cook, I make all my own meals. My favourite recipes include soups, vegetable dishes and shortbread. I often adapt traditional recipes, such as salad dressings, pancakes and falafels, so they fit in with the detox rules. I normally make the recipes up for four people and freeze the rest, so I have enough for the month!

The best thing about the detox diet is that the food is lovely. I never feel hungry. And I never get bored with the meals, as there are so many ways to use seasonal vegetables, fruit and grains. It can be hard going out for meals and to parties but I just get back to my normal diet the next day.

My family all eat organic food, where possible, now. I am always aware of what I am eating now and have become a bit of a "preacher" to friends and family!

I recently had my blood cholesterol level checked and the results are great. The good type (HDL) is high and the bad type (LDL) is low, which means I have below-average risk for having a stroke or heart attack. My doctor is full of awe! At 56 and weighing 9½ stone I put my good health all down to my diet. Thank you.'

Lisa Richardson, 34, office manager

'I decided to start the detox after several friends had done it and reported excellent results.

I wanted to lose weight and feel healthier but I was sceptical that the detox diet would work for me. I loved my food too much and imagined that I would be hungry.

But I was wrong. I would have a mango, banana and almond milk smoothie for breakfast (from Detox for Life) and not feel hungry until lunchtime. I loved eating salad with cashew nuts, sunflower seeds and rye bread for lunch. On the few occasions I did feel hungry between meals, a couple of Brazil nuts were enough to stave off the hunger. I found I was able to eat when I was hungry instead of eating by the clock.

My cravings for crisps and chocolate and Mini Cheddars disappeared. The key to beating those cravings was to stock my cupboard with all the right ingredients – no 'naughty' foods allowed – so that I could follow the recipes. My favourite foods were almond milk, avocados, unsalted cashew nuts, and roasted vegetables with pasta and asparagus. I liked the fact that – unlike most weight-loss diets – you don't have to weigh any of the food. I also switched to eating from a smaller plate. Previously I had eaten from a big plate and had seconds. With the detox diet, I found sometimes I could not even clear the small plate!

The hardest thing was giving up cheese and alcohol. I did get headaches at the start due to giving up coffee and diet coke but these soon stopped.

My self-esteem has benefited greatly. After trying to control what I ate for most of my life, I never would have thought a diet plan would have such profound effects. People have noticed how good I look and so far that has encouraged several of my work colleagues to try the plan. They report similar results! I lost 10lb in 28 days and that has spurred me on to continue. A skin rash on my hands has 90% disappeared; my skin is clearer; my breath smells nicer and teeth feel cleaner. I feel full and satisfied for hours after meals. All in all I am much happier now that I am more in control of my eating.'

John Scott, 43, TV presenter and stylist, fashion expert on ITV's This Morning

'The reason I chose the Detox Diet is because I'm vegetarian – I don't eat any meat, or fish, and I don't have dairy products either, as I'm actually intolerant of those. As a younger person, I suffered from really bad Irritable Bowl Syndrome and since I'm not supposed to have coffee, sugar, chocolate, or things like that, I live with a perpetually grumbly tummy, whereas when I'm on the Detox Diet, there's no problem whatsoever, no sign of that. You feel so much better and you have so much more energy.

Really, I went on the Detox Diet literally to detox, not to diet – I wanted to clear my system out because I was feeling 'fuggy'. And it seemed the perfect one to do. The food itself is good because it's what's in my cupboard. All I have to do is clear out the biscuits and the cakes and the coffee, all the junk food that I do like to eat. As far as the rest of it goes, it's actually the things I'd eat anyway. For example, hummus is my favourite food and you can eat as much hummus as you like!

The first time I did it, I lost two and a half stones. Then I did it six months later and I lost a stone, and each time I do the normal monthly version, I usually lose a stone. But the very first time I did it, I didn't break any rules whatsoever. I just followed the diet, whereas when I do it now, I do cheat a little bit but I still lose weight and I still feel better for it.

From day two it starts working, clearing your system out, so there's not a problem, although I had really, really bad headaches to begin with. Since then the headaches have been nowhere near as bad. Almost on the dot a week later, I woke up in the morning and felt so fantastic. My energy levels were up and my skin was clearer and people were noticing. You might not feel as though you've lost anything – in fact, for the first ten days no weight moved at all – and I know Carol says "Don't weigh yourself", but I was weighing myself and nothing happened for the first week and then suddenly it disappeared from nowhere. I started losing the weight on a regular basis. The thing is I know what it's like to do it now and I know it's worth doing it because you do feel so fabulous at the end of it all.

CHAPTER 3
WHAT TO EAT

ABOUT THE RECIPES

If you enjoyed the meals in the 28-day Detox for Life or the 14-day mini Summer Detox, you will definitely love the recipes we've created for you in this book. They follow the same detox principles, of course, and taste absolutely delicious.

If you are new to the detox diet, the recipes in this book will hopefully inspire you to a new healthy way of eating. They show you how easy it is to prepare healthy meals that fit perfectly into your lifestyle.

Hundreds of thousands of people in the UK have now tried the detox and love it. But many of you have asked what to do after the first 28 days. And here is the answer. There are two sets of recipes: one set is marked with the symbol **D** for the strict detox and the other set marked **M** for maintenance.

The **D** (detox) recipes in this book follow all the detox rules – no meat, fish, dairy, wheat, sugar or eggs – and are especially rich in vitamins, minerals and other 'detox' nutrients. Use them as part of the detox diet or whenever you want a healthy boost.

The **M** (maintenance) recipes are a little less strict and may include poultry, fish or low-fat dairy products. They are still well balanced but give you a little more room for manoeuvre. Use them for everyday eating or entertaining.

Some of the detox recipes have a symbol **O** with optional ingredients that can be included when you are not on a strict detox diet or when you are cooking for other people.

The dishes are simple and quick to prepare and you don't have to be a great cook! The quantities serve four, but you can adapt them by changing the quantities if you want.

All of the recipes in this book make use of the fantastic fresh produce available from supermarkets, markets and corner shops. There's no need to buy anything from specialist shops. The main thing is to choose the freshest and best-quality foods you can find. Buy seasonal and locally grown produce if you can, visit local markets and if time allows, try to shop little and often for fresh produce so you get the most goodness from them.

Enjoy!

HOW TO MAKE THE DETOX DIET WORK FOR YOU

1. **Eat food as close to its natural state as possible**
2. **Avoid processed foods**
3. **Drink 6–8 glasses of water daily**
4. **Eat at least 5 portions of fruit and vegetables each day**
5. **Eat when you are hungry – never starve**
6. **Make your skin glow by dry skin brushing daily before bathing**

THE DETOX RULES

The detox diet is about eating nutrient-packed fresh food and ditching processed foods, sugar, salt and additives. The vitamins, minerals, antioxidants and fibre in fresh food restore your body to peak health, aid digestion and boost your immunity.

What to eat D

- Fresh fruit
- Vegetables
- Salad
- Unrefined non-wheat cereals – wholegrain (brown) rice, oats, millet, quinoa, rye, buckwheat
- Non-wheat bread – rye bread, wheat-free, pumpernickel
- Non-wheat pasta – corn, millet or rice pasta
- Non-wheat crispbreads – rye, rice cakes, oatcakes
- Water, herbal or fruit tea, pure fruit juice
- Beans, lentils and peas
- Tofu and quorn
- Non-dairy milk – soya, rice, oat, almond or sesame 'milk'
- Nuts – almonds, cashews, hazelnuts, brazils, pecans, peanuts
- Seeds – pumpkin, sunflower, sesame, ground flaxseeds (linseeds)
- Extra virgin olive oil, rapeseed, walnut, flaxseed (linseed) or sesame oil
- Cold-pressed oil blends containing a mixture of omega-3-rich and omega-6-rich oils
- Fresh herbs

Maintenance M

- Low-fat yoghurt and fromage frais
- Skimmed or semi-skimmed milk
- Cottage cheese and other low-fat cheeses
- Wholemeal bread
- Wholegrain breakfast cereals
- Chicken, turkey and lean meat
- White fish and oily fish

What to avoid on a strict detox

- Coffee, tea and other caffeine drinks (including decaffeinated drinks)
- Dairy products – milk, cheese, yoghurt, cream
- Sugar
- Cakes, biscuits, confectionery
- Meat
- Fish
- Eggs
- Wheat bread, pasta, noodles, crackers
- White rice
- Ready meals
- Salt
- Alcohol
- Artificial food additives
- Fried foods
- Artificial sweeteners
- Hydrogenated fats
- Fizzy drinks
- Squashes and cordials

CHAPTER 4
FOOD FOR HEALTH

Detoxing is not about starving yourself, counting calories or obsessively weighing yourself. It's about eating healthily and enjoying tasty meals that help your natural detox system work properly and balance your body. It means limiting the amount of toxins you consume – artificial additives, caffeine, alcohol, salt and sugar – and eating instead nutrient-packed fresh foods. Here are ten good reasons to eat the detox way:

1. **You'll lose excess weight**

2. **Cellulite will diminish**

3. **You'll feel more energetic**

4. **You'll get fewer colds**

5. **You'll get rid of bloating**

6. **Your skin will look smoother**

7. **You'll enjoy better health**

8. **Your hair will shine**

9. **You'll feel calmer**

10. **You can lower blood pressure and bad cholesterol**

CARBOHYDRATES, PROTEIN AND FAT

Your body needs the right proportions of carbohydrates, proteins and good fats to keep healthy. Carbohydrates are an important energy source for your brain as well as your muscles. The recipes in this book feature the fibre-rich carbohydrates – whole grains, wheat-free pasta, fruit, vegetables, beans and low-fat dairy foods – that produce a slower and longer-lasting energy release.

Protein is the building block of your body and is needed to continuously rebuild and repair the tissues. Without enough protein, body maintenance slows down and you'll lose muscle tone. In the detox recipes you can get protein from non-meat sources: beans, lentils, nuts, seeds, soya, tofu, quorn and grains. It is important to eat a variety of these foods so that your body gets what it needs.

It is important to include healthy fats in your daily fats. They help release energy from food, strengthen the immune system and promote healthier skin and hair. They are the unsaturated fats: monounsaturated fats (olive oil and rapeseed oil), omega-3 fats (oily fish, walnuts, pumpkin seeds, flaxseed oil), and omega-6 fats (sunflower oil, nuts and seeds). Try to include one tablespoon of an omega-3-rich oil or a heaped tablespoon of nuts or seeds daily.

VITAMINS, MINERALS AND ANTIOXIDANTS

Your body needs vitamins to convert food into energy, maintain healthy skin, blood and nerves, and to help the immune system work properly. Minerals are needed for healthy bones and teeth, transporting nutrients to cells, balancing body fluids and controlling energy production.

Antioxidant nutrients include vitamins C and E, betacarotene, selenium, zinc and phytonutrients (beneficial plant nutrients). They help to protect the body from the harmful effects of free radicals, boost the immune system and keep you in good health. Diets rich in antioxidants help prevent heart disease, certain cancers, cataracts and premature ageing.

You'll find vitamins, minerals and antioxidants in abundance in fruit, vegetables, beans, lentils, whole grains, nuts and seeds – foods that feature heavily in the detox recipes. Try to eat at least 5 portions of fruit and vegetables daily.

While following a detox diet you may wish to take daily multivitamin/mineral and antioxidant supplements. You may also benefit from a milk thistle supplement, which supports the detoxification processes in the liver. A more detailed explanation of the 28-day detox diet can be found in *Carol Vorderman's Detox for Life*; and a 14-day mini detox diet is featured in *Carol Vorderman's Summer Detox*.

SNACKS

Healthy snacking helps to ward off energy highs and lows. Have a mid-morning and mid-afternoon snack – or when you feel hungry. Try the following or any of the new recipes on pages 61–77:

- An apple, pear or satsuma
- A bunch of grapes
- A banana
- A plum or apricot
- Vegetable crudités with hummus or avocado dip
- A few cashews, almonds, peanuts or walnuts
- Some raisins or other variety of dried fruit
- A small handful of sunflower, pumpkin or sesame seeds
- A glass of juice
- A smoothie
- Rice cakes, oatcakes or rye crispbreads with peanut butter or hummus

WATER

Drinking plenty of water helps flush toxins from your system. It also rebalances your body fluids, reduces water retention and bloating, prevents constipation and gives you healthier looking skin. Aim to drink 6–8 glasses of water daily. Count herbal and fruit tea, decaffeinated coffee and tea, green tea and fruit juice towards your daily target.

ORGANIC CHOICE

Choosing organic food will go a long way towards reducing your intake of toxins – pesticide residues, antibiotics, nitrates and hormones – but the price of organic food means that it isn't always realistic. If you can't eat organic all the time, just concentrate on organic versions of salads and fruit, especially berries and soft fruit, as these foods are the most heavily sprayed and have the highest pesticide residue content. For other fruits and vegetables, wash them thoroughly in water or remove the peel.

It can be hard to find ready made products in supermarkets which you can eat safe in the knowledge that they're approved for detox and totally natural. I can thoroughly recommend Simply Organic. A small company which makes excellent ranges of 'convenient without compromise' fresh organic soups, sauces and 'Pure and Pronto' ready meals – all of which are organic and many of which are also suitable for detox. Simply Organic ranges are stocked in supermarkets and good independent stores. Call Simply Organic on 0131 4480440 for further information and stockists.

A healthy diet for maintenance should be enjoyable, delicious and also be good for you. Try to stick to the 80/20 rule, which means that you stick to the detox rules around 80% of the time, while the other 20% of the time you are free to enjoy other foods you want.

CHAPTER 5
TOP 12 DETOX FOODS

APPLES

Apples contain vitamin C – a great immune booster – and quercetin, an antioxidant that protects against cancer. Apples are also rich in pectin, a soluble type of fibre that helps lower blood-cholesterol levels and keeps the intestines and bowel working properly.

AVOCADOS

Avocados are rich in vitamin E and alphacarotene, both powerful antioxidants that help prevent furring of the arteries and heart disease. They also contain monounsaturated fat, which lowers blood cholesterol and heart disease risk, as well as the essential omega-6 fats, which promote healthy skin.

BEANS AND LENTILS

Beans and lentils contain a good balance of protein and complex carbohydrates, and provide sustained energy. They are rich in sterols (plant compounds) and soluble fibre, both of which help lower blood cholesterol, as well as B-vitamins, magnesium, zinc and iron.

BROCCOLI

Broccoli along with other cruciferous vegetables – cauliflower, cabbage, Brussels sprouts and spinach – are powerful detoxifiers. They contain phytonutrients called glucosinolates, which can fight cancer, especially of the bowel, breast, lungs and liver.

CARROTS

Carrots are rich in the antioxidants, alphacarotene and betacarotene, which help to protect against lung cancer. These nutrients also help to boost immunity, promote healthier skin and maintain good eyesight.

FENNEL

Fennel helps stimulate the body's natural detoxifying organs, including the liver. It is also good for the digestive system and its high potassium content helps rebalance the body's fluid levels.

GARLIC

Garlic contains allicin, an antioxidant nutrient that helps protect the body from heart disease, high blood pressure, high blood-cholesterol levels and colon cancer. It can also bind with toxins in the body to render them harmless and promote their excretion. It also has antiviral and antibacterial actions.

KIWI FRUIT

Kiwi fruit are super-rich in vitamin C, an antioxidant that helps fight cancer and potentially harmful free radicals. It also boosts the immune system and strengthens the blood vessels.

MANGO

Mangoes are rich in betacarotene and vitamin C, two powerful antioxidants that help ward off colds and reduce the risk of cancer and heart disease. They are also good sources of vitamin E, fibre and potassium.

PUMPKIN SEEDS

Pumpkin seeds and their oil contain a healthy balance of the essential omega-3 and omega-6 oils, which help to protect against heart disease and stroke. Omega-3-rich foods can reduce joint pain and stiffness, improve immunity and promote healthy skin.

STRAWBERRIES

Strawberries are rich in vitamin C. Just five strawberries provide an adult's daily requirement for this vitamin, which not only boosts immunity but also fights free radicals and helps prevent heart disease and cancer. Strawberries are rich in the antioxidant, ellagic acid, which has powerful anticancer effects.

WATERCRESS

Watercress is rich in chlorophyll, a dark green pigment, which helps make healthy blood cells and boosts circulation. It boosts levels of detoxifying enzymes in the liver. Watercress is rich in vitamin C, iron and betacarotene and is good for improving immunity and heart health.

CHAPTER 6
BREAKFASTS

Eating breakfast not only fuels your body for the day but is also good for the brain. Choose from delicious cereal grains, fresh fruit, dried fruit or homemade pancakes to boost your energy and sharpen your concentration. Its been proven that breakfast eaters are healthier, slimmer and happier. So what are you waiting for?

BANANA PORRIDGE WITH HONEY

MAKES 4 SERVINGS
175 G (6 OZ) ROLLED PORRIDGE OATS
250 ML (9 FL OZ) SOYA, RICE, SESAME OR ALMOND MILK
250 ML (9 FL OZ) WATER
1–2 TABLESPOONS (15–30 ML) LINSEED (FLAXSEED) OIL (OPTIONAL)
4 TABLESPOONS (60 ML) RAISINS
2 TABLESPOONS (30 ML) GROUND ALMONDS
1 TABLESPOON (15 ML) TOASTED PUMPKIN SEEDS
2 BANANAS, PEELED AND SLICED
1 TABLESPOON (15 ML) HONEY

Mix the oats, milk and water in a saucepan. Bring to the boil and simmer for 4–5 minutes, stirring frequently.

Stir in the linseed (flaxseed) oil (if using), raisins, almonds and seeds.

Spoon into bowls and serve topped with the sliced banana and honey.

O **You may substitute skimmed milk for the non-dairy milk.**

D

HEALTH STATISTICS
Oats are rich in soluble fibre – excellent for improving digestion and lowering blood cholesterol – as well as magnesium and zinc. They provide slow-release energy to sustain your energy levels through the morning. The almonds and seeds provide essential fats to help balance hormone levels and promote healthy-looking skin.

MILLET OR RICE PORRIDGE WITH HONEY

MAKES 4 SERVINGS
175 G (6 OZ) MILLET FLAKES
225 ML (9 FL OZ) SOYA, RICE, OAT OR ALMOND MILK
225 ML (9 FL OZ) WATER
A FEW DROPS OF VANILLA EXTRACT, TO TASTE
2 TABLESPOONS (30 ML) GROUND LINSEEDS (FLAXSEEDS)
4 TEASPOONS (20 ML) CLEAR HONEY

Mix the millet, milk and water in a saucepan. Bring to the boil and simmer for 4–5 minutes, stirring continuously.

Stir in the vanilla extract and ground linseeds (flaxseeds). Serve with the honey.

O **You may substitute skimmed milk for the non-dairy milk.**

D

HEALTH STATISTICS
Millet is a good source of magnesium and iron. The linseeds are super-rich in omega-3 fatty acids, fibre and are excellent for maintaining a healthy gut.

MUESLI WITH FRESH FRUIT

MAKES 4 SERVINGS

175 G (6 OZ) MIXTURE OF OATS, MILLET FLAKES AND RYE FLAKES
300 ML (1/2 PINT) SOYA, RICE, ALMOND OR OAT MILK
2 TABLESPOONS (30 ML) EACH OF TOASTED SUNFLOWER SEEDS AND PUMPKIN SEEDS
60 G (2 OZ) TOASTED FLAKED ALMONDS
350–400 G (12–14 OZ) FRESH FRUIT, E.G. CHOPPED MANGO, SLICED BANANAS, STRAWBERRIES, RASPBERRIES OR BLUEBERRIES

Place the cereal flakes in a bowl and pour the milk over them. Leave to soak for at least 2 hours (preferably overnight) in the fridge.

Stir in the seeds and almonds. Serve in individual bowls, topped with the fresh fruit.

O **You may substitute skimmed milk for the non-dairy milk.**

D

HEALTH STATISTICS
Oat and rye flakes are rich in soluble fibre, good for regulating blood sugar and insulin levels and reducing cholesterol levels. They also supply B-vitamins, iron, magnesium and zinc. The seeds provide omega-3 and omega-6 fatty acids, to help balance hormone levels and promote overall good health. And the fresh fruit is rich in vitamin C, betacarotene and fibre.

GRANOLA

MAKES 4 SERVINGS
225 G (8 OZ) OATS
60 G (2 OZ) SUNFLOWER SEEDS
60 G (2 OZ) FLAKED ALMONDS
60 G (2 OZ) HAZELNUTS, CRUSHED
2 TABLESPOONS (30 ML) CLEAR HONEY
2 TABLESPOONS (30 ML) RAPESEED OIL
85 ML (3 FL OZ) WATER
1 TEASPOON (5 ML) VANILLA EXTRACT
1 TEASPOON GROUND CINNAMON
1 TEASPOON GROUND GINGER
A PINCH OF GROUND ALLSPICE (OPTIONAL)
85 G (3 OZ) CHOPPED DATES, RAISINS OR APRICOTS (OR A MIXTURE)

Heat the oven to 190°C/375°F/Gas mark 5.

Mix the oats, sunflower seeds, almonds and hazelnuts together
in a bowl.

In a separate bowl, combine the honey, oil, water, vanilla and spices.
Add to the oat mixture and mix well.

Spread out on a nonstick baking tray and bake in the oven for
30–40 minutes, stirring occasionally until evenly browned.

Cool and then mix in the dried fruit. Store in an airtight container.
Serve with skimmed, soya, rice or oat milk, natural yoghurt and/
or fresh fruit.

D

HEALTH STATISTICS
Oats are rich in soluble fibre and
provide slow-release energy as
well as plenty of B-vitamins and
iron. Almonds and hazelnuts both
provide protein, calcium, zinc and
healthy monounsaturated oils.

DRIED FRUIT COMPOTE WITH VANILLA AND ORANGE

MAKES 4 SERVINGS

1 ORANGE
2 TABLESPOONS (30 ML) ACACIA HONEY
300 ML (1/2 PINT) WATER
150 ML (5 FL OZ) ORANGE JUICE

1 VANILLA POD, HALVED LENGTHWISE
85 G (3 OZ) DRIED FIGS, HALVED
85 G (3 OZ) DRIED APRICOTS
85 G (3 OZ) PITTED PRUNES

Peel the zest in long strips from the orange with a vegetable peeler and cut into thin julienne strips. Halve the orange and squeeze the juice.

Combine the zest, freshly squeezed juice, honey, water and orange juice in a saucepan.

Scrape the seeds from the vanilla pod with a sharp knife and add to the pan, reserving the pod for another use.

Bring mixture to the boil, stirring until the honey is dissolved, then add the dried fruit and simmer, covered, for about 15 minutes until they become plump and soft. Allow to cool and keep covered in the fridge until you are ready to serve.

HEALTH STATISTICS
Dried fruit is super-rich in soluble fibre, which helps balance blood sugar levels, reduce cholesterol levels and promote healthy digestion. Figs are also rich in calcium and the dried apricots supply betacarotene and iron. Prunes have one of the highest antioxidant scores of all fruits.

MUESLI WITH APPLE AND SULTANAS

MAKES 4 SERVINGS

175 G (6 OZ) MIXTURE OF OATS, MILLET FLAKES AND RYE FLAKES
300 ML (1/2 PINT) SOYA, RICE, ALMOND OR OAT MILK
2 TABLESPOONS (30 ML) SULTANAS
2 TABLESPOONS (30 ML) MIXTURE OF GROUND LINSEEDS (FLAXSEEDS), SUNFLOWER AND PUMPKIN SEEDS
2 TABLESPOONS (30 ML) HONEY
2 TABLESPOONS (30 ML) LEMON JUICE
2 APPLES, GRATED

In a large bowl, mix together the oats, milk, sultanas and ground seeds. Cover and leave for at least 2 hours (preferably overnight) in the fridge.

Stir in the honey, lemon juice and grated apple, and then serve.

You may substitute skimmed milk for the non-dairy milk and stir in 3–4 tablespoons of natural bio-yoghurt just before serving.

HEALTH STATISTICS
Oat and rye flakes are rich in soluble fibre, good for regulating blood sugar and insulin levels and reducing cholesterol levels. They also supply B-vitamins, iron, magnesium and zinc. The seed mixture provides a near-perfect balance of omega-3 and omega-6 fatty acids, to help balance hormone levels and promote overall good health. Apples are great intestinal cleansers.

PANCAKES WITH FRESH FRUIT

MAKES 10–12 PANCAKES

PANCAKES:
70 G (2 OZ) PLAIN WHITE FLOUR
70 G (2 OZ) PLAIN WHOLEMEAL FLOUR
2 EGGS
250 ML (8 FL OZ) SOYA, RICE, ALMOND, OAT OR SKIMMED MILK
A LITTLE RAPESEED OIL OR OIL SPRAY FOR FRYING

FILLING:
SLICED BANANAS, SLICED STRAWBERRIES, APPLE PUREE WITH
RAISINS, LIGHTLY CRUSHED RASPBERRIES, FROZEN BERRY MIXTURE
(THAWED), CHOPPED MANGO, OR SLICED NECTARINES OR PEACHES
NATURAL BIO-YOGHURT, TO SERVE

Place the flours, eggs and milk in a liquidiser and blend to make a smooth batter.

Heat a nonstick frying pan over a high heat. Spray with oil spray or add a few drops of oil. Pour in enough batter to coat the pan thinly and cook for 1–2 minutes until golden brown on the underside.

Turn the pancake and cook the other side for 30–60 seconds.

Turn out on a plate, cover and keep warm while you make the other pancakes.

Serve with any of the suggested fresh fruit fillings and bio-yoghurt.

HEALTH STATISTICS
The eggs and milk are good sources of protein. The milk is rich in calcium and the fruit fillings provide vitamin C, betacarotene and fibre.

CHAPTER 7
SOUPS

Health-boosting soups must be one of the easiest ways of supplying your body with vital nutrients. From hearty warming soups like Spicy Parsnip and Root vegetables to cooling summer soups like Gazpacho and Mediterranean Summer vegetable, you'll find delicious soups to revitalise your body and rejuvenate your mind.

VEGETABLE STOCK

MAKES 600 ML (1 PINT)

900 ML (1½ PINTS) WATER

2 ONIONS, SLICED

2 CARROTS, ROUGHLY SLICED

2 CELERY STICKS, HALVED

1 LEEK, HALVED

2 BAY LEAVES

2 SPRIGS OF THYME

2 SPRIGS OF PARSLEY

8 BLACK PEPPERCORNS

PINCH OF SEA SALT TO SEASON

Put the water, vegetables, herbs and seasonings in a large saucepan.

Bring to the boil and simmer gently for at least 1 hour. Leave to cool and then strain.

D

Use this stock for making soups, stews and casseroles in any recipes that call for stock. Alternatively, use 4 teaspoons (20 ml) low-sodium vegetable bouillon powder dissolved in 1 litre of hot water.

MEDITERRANEAN SUMMER VEGETABLE SOUP

MAKES 4 SERVINGS

1 TABLESPOON (15 ML) EXTRA VIRGIN OLIVE OIL
1 ONION, THINLY SLICED
2 GARLIC CLOVES, FINELY CHOPPED
1 RED PEPPER, DESEEDED AND SLICED
1 GREEN PEPPER, DESEEDED AND SLICED
2 COURGETTES, TRIMMED AND SLICED
450 G (1 LB) TOMATOES, SKINNED AND QUARTERED
HALF AN AUBERGINE, DICED
1 LITRE (1 3/4 PINTS) VEGETABLE STOCK OR WATER
A LITTLE LOW-SODIUM SALT, TO TASTE
4 TEASPOONS (20 ML) PESTO

Heat the olive oil in a large saucepan. Add the onion and garlic and sauté over a moderate heat for about 5 minutes until it is translucent.

Add the prepared vegetables, stock or water, and then bring to the boil. Simmer for about 25–30 minutes or until the vegetables are tender.

Allow the soup to cool slightly for a couple of minutes. Liquidise the soup using a hand blender or conventional blender. Season to taste with the low-sodium salt.

Serve in individual bowls, adding a teaspoon of pesto to each bowl immediately before serving.

HEALTH STATISTICS
This dish is rich in vitamin C (from the tomatoes and peppers), betacarotene and lycopene (both from the tomatoes), a powerful antioxidant that helps to protect against heart disease and several cancers. It is also an excellent source of potassium, good for regulating fluid balance and controlling blood pressure.

ROOT VEGETABLE SOUP

MAKES 4 SERVINGS

1 TABLESPOON (15 ML) EXTRA VIRGIN OLIVE OIL
1 ONION, FINELY SLICED
450 G (1 LB) (APPROX 6) CARROTS, SLICED
225 G (8 OZ) (APPROX 2) PARSNIPS, DICED
225 G (8 OZ) SWEDE, DICED
1 LITRE (1³/4 PINTS) VEGETABLE STOCK
1 BAY LEAF
A LITTLE LOW-SODIUM SALT AND FRESHLY GROUND BLACK PEPPER

Heat the olive oil in a heavy-based saucepan over a moderate heat. Add the onion and sauté gently for about 5 minutes until it is translucent.

Add the carrots, parsnips and swede to the pan and mix well. Cook gently over a moderately low heat for 5 minutes, stirring occasionally, until the vegetables soften a little.

Add the stock and bay leaf and bring to the boil. Simmer for 15 minutes or until the vegetables are tender.

Allow the soup to cool slightly for a couple of minutes. Remove and discard the bay leaf. Liquidise the soup using a hand blender or conventional blender. Season to taste with salt and pepper.

D

HEALTH STATISTICS
Carrots are super-rich in betacarotene, a powerful antioxidant that helps prevent cancer, beat premature ageing and promotes healthy skin. All of the vegetables are rich in potassium, the parsnips provide good amounts of vitamin E and swede is a good source of vitamin C.

SPRING VEGETABLE SOUP

MAKES 4 SERVINGS

2 TABLESPOONS (30 ML) EXTRA VIRGIN OLIVE OIL

2 LEEKS, FINELY SLICED

1½ LITRES (2½ PINTS) VEGETABLE STOCK

125 G SMALL WHEAT-FREE PASTA SHAPES

125 G (4 OZ) SUGAR-SNAP PEAS, HALVED LENGTHWAYS

125 G (4 OZ) FINE GREEN BEANS, TOPPED, TAILED AND HALVED

125 G (4 OZ) FROZEN PEAS

2 COURGETTES, TRIMMED AND SLICED

A SMALL HANDFUL OF BASIL LEAVES, ROUGHLY TORN

A LITTLE LOW-SODIUM SALT AND FRESHLY GROUND BLACK PEPPER

Heat the olive oil in a large heavy-based saucepan. Add the leeks and gently sauté for about 10 minutes or until the leeks have softened, but not coloured.

Pour in the stock and bring to the boil. Add the pasta and simmer for 2 minutes.

Add the sugar-snaps and green beans and cook for 1 minute. Add the peas and courgettes and simmer for a further 2 minutes. Stir in the basil and season with low-sodium salt and freshly ground pepper.

O **Top with shavings of Parmesan cheese.**

D

HEALTH STATISTICS

This soup is a good source of potassium – important for controlling high blood pressure – and the sugar snaps are super-rich in vitamin C. The vegetables also provide folate – useful for reducing the risk of arteriosclerosis – as well as useful amounts of fibre.

PEA AND MINT SOUP

MAKES 4 SERVINGS

2 TABLESPOONS (30 ML) EXTRA VIRGIN OLIVE OIL

1 SMALL ONION, FINELY CHOPPED

450 G (1 LB) FROZEN PETITS POIS

900 ML (1½ PINTS) VEGETABLE STOCK

A SMALL HANDFUL OF FRESH MINT LEAVES

Heat the olive oil in a large heavy-based saucepan, add the chopped onion and cook over a low heat for 5 minutes until the onion is translucent.

Add the peas, vegetable stock and half of the mint leaves. Cover and simmer for 5 minutes.

Liquidise the soup, using a hand blender or conventional blender, with the remaining mint leaves until smooth.

Reheat gently.

0 **Serve with a swirl of natural whole milk or Greek yoghurt.**

D

HEALTH STATISTICS

Peas supply protein as well as carbohydrate. They are also rich in fibre, iron and vitamin C. Mint is an excellent digestive aid as well as a super-rich source of iron, vitamin E and folate.

CALDO VERDE

MAKES 4 SERVINGS
2 TABLESPOONS (30 ML) EXTRA VIRGIN OLIVE OIL
1 LARGE ONION, CHOPPED
2 GARLIC CLOVES, CRUSHED
450 G (1 LB) POTATOES, PEELED AND DICED
1 LITRE (1³/₄ PINTS) VEGETABLE STOCK
450 G (1 LB) SAVOY CABBAGE OR SPRING GREENS, FINELY SHREDDED
A LITTLE LOW-SODIUM SALT AND FRESHLY GROUND BLACK PEPPER, TO TASTE

Heat the olive oil in a large heavy-based pan and cook the onion, garlic and potatoes over a moderate heat for about 5 minutes.

Add the stock and shredded cabbage, bring to the boil, and then simmer for 20 minutes until the vegetables are tender.

Remove half of the soup and liquidise using a hand blender or conventional blender. Return to the pan, stir well and reheat for a minute or two until piping hot. Season with salt and black pepper.

D
HEALTH STATISTICS
Savoy cabbage is rich in vitamin C and betacarotene, which are both good immune boosters. The outer green leaves of cabbage contain as much as 50 times the vitamins as inner white ones.

BROCCOLI SOUP

MAKES 4 SERVINGS
450 G (1 LB) BROCCOLI FLORETS
1 ONION, CHOPPED
450 ML (³/₄ PINT) VEGETABLE STOCK
450 ML (³/₄ PINT) SKIMMED OR NON-DAIRY MILK
2 TEASPOONS (10 ML) CORNFLOUR, BLENDED WITH A LITTLE WATER
A LITTLE LOW-SODIUM SALT AND FRESHLY GROUND BLACK PEPPER TO TASTE
40 G (1¹/₂ OZ) TOASTED FLAKED ALMONDS

Place the onion, broccoli and vegetable stock in a saucepan. Bring to the boil and simmer for about 15 minutes until the vegetables are soft.

Liquidise the soup using a hand blender or food processor.

Return to the saucepan with the milk, and then stir in the cornflour blended with a little water. Bring to the boil, stirring, and then simmer gently for a minute or two.

Serve in individual bowls, sprinkling each portion with the toasted almonds.

M
HEALTH STATISTICS
Broccoli is rich in sulphoraphane, a powerful anticancer compound that reduces the risk of cancer of the bowel, stomach, breast and lungs. It's also rich in vitamin C, folate and fibre. This soup is also a good source of protein and calcium (from the milk) and the flaked almonds provide vitamin E, iron, zinc and further calcium.

GAZPACHO

MAKES 4 SERVINGS

675 G (1½ LB) TOMATOES, SKINNED AND QUARTERED

2 GARLIC CLOVES, ROUGHLY SLICED

1 RED PEPPER, DESEEDED AND CUT INTO QUARTERS

1 SMALL RED ONION, ROUGHLY CHOPPED

HALF A CUCUMBER, ROUGHLY CHOPPED

2 TABLESPOONS (30 ML) TOMATO PASTE

1 TEASPOON (5 ML) SUGAR, OR TO TASTE

2 TABLESPOONS (30 ML) EXTRA VIRGIN OLIVE OIL

3 TABLESPOONS (30 ML) SHERRY VINEGAR OR WINE VINEGAR

A LITTLE LOW-SODIUM SALT AND FRESHLY GROUND BLACK
PEPPER, TO TASTE

2 SLICES WHEAT-FREE WHITE BREAD, CRUSTS REMOVED

GARNISH:

HALF A CUCUMBER, FINELY DICED

HALF A RED ONION, FINELY CHOPPED

HALF A GREEN PEPPER, FINELY DICED

Place all of the ingredients in a large bowl and mix together.
Blend in two batches in a food processor or blender. Add a little
cold water – about 150 ml (5 fl oz) – to thin it, if necessary.

Taste the soup and adjust the seasoning with a little more vinegar,
salt, pepper or sugar.

Return to the bowl, cover and chill for at least an hour before
serving. Stir before serving accompanied by individual dishes
of the garnish ingredients.

O **Use ordinary (wheat) bread instead of the wheat-free bread,
if you wish. You may use chopped hard-boiled egg or croutons
to accompany the soup as well.**

D

HEALTH STATISTICS
This soup is super-rich in vitamin
C, a terrific immune booster
that's also good for your skin.
The tomatoes are also rich in
betacarotene and lycopene, both
powerful anticancer nutrients.
As the soup is uncooked, there
is minimal loss of vitamins.

THAI CHICKEN AND COCONUT

MAKES 4 SERVINGS
2 CHICKEN BREASTS CUT INTO STRIPS
ZEST AND JUICE OF 1 LIME
400 ML (14 FL OZ) COCONUT MILK
400 ML (14 FL OZ) HOT CHICKEN OR VEGETABLE STOCK
1 STEM OF LEMON GRASS, CUT INTO STRIPS
2.5 CM (1 IN) FRESH GINGER, PEELED AND GRATED
1 RED CHILLI, FINELY CHOPPED (OPTIONAL)
2 TABLESPOONS (30 ML) CHOPPED FRESH CORIANDER LEAVES

In a shallow dish, sprinkle the lime juice over the chicken pieces, cover and leave to marinate in the fridge for at least 30 minutes.

Place the remaining ingredients in a large saucepan and heat until boiling. Add the chicken pieces and lime juice. Reduce the heat and simmer for 15 minutes.

Ladle into 4 bowls and sprinkle over the coriander leaves.

M

HEALTH STATISTICS
Chicken is rich in protein and B-vitamins. The ginger and chillies stimulate the immune system.

SPICED LENTIL SOUP WITH CARROTS

MAKES 4 SERVINGS
1 TABLESPOON (15 ML) EXTRA VIRGIN OLIVE OIL
1 ONION, CHOPPED
2 GARLIC CLOVES, CRUSHED
1 TEASPOON (5 ML) GROUND CUMIN
1 TEASPOON (5 ML) GROUND CORIANDER
2 CARROTS, SLICED
150 G (5 OZ) RED LENTILS
1 LITRE (1³/₄ PINTS) VEGETABLE STOCK
A LITTLE LOW-SODIUM SALT AND FRESHLY GROUND BLACK
PEPPER TO TASTE
JUICE OF HALF A LEMON

Heat the olive oil in a large saucepan. Add the onion and sauté over a moderate heat for about 5 minutes until soft, stirring occasionally.

Stir in the garlic, cumin and coriander and cook for 1 minute, stirring continuously. Add the carrots, lentils and stock. Bring to the boil and skim off any scum that appears on the surface. Reduce the heat and simmer for about 30–35 minutes until the lentils are very mushy.

Season with salt and black pepper and thin with a little water if necessary. Add the lemon juice before serving.

D

HEALTH STATISTICS
Red lentils contain an excellent balance of protein and complex carbohydrate as well as soluble fibre, iron and B-vitamins. They provide sustained energy, due to the soluble fibre content. The carrots are super-rich in betacarotene, which helps to protect the body from cancer and benefits the skin.

LEEK AND POTATO SOUP

MAKES 4 SERVINGS
1 LITRE (1³/₄ PINTS) VEGETABLE STOCK
3 MEDIUM POTATOES, SCRUBBED AND ROUGHLY CHOPPED
3 LARGE LEEKS, SLICED
1 LARGE CARROT, SLICED
A LITTLE LOW-SODIUM SALT AND FRESHLY GROUND BLACK PEPPER
A SMALL HANDFUL OF CHOPPED FRESH PARSLEY

Place the vegetable stock, potatoes, leeks and carrots in a large saucepan. Bring to the boil, lower the heat, cover and simmer for about 20 minutes until the vegetables are tender.

Remove from the heat and liquidise until smooth using a blender, food processor or a hand blender.

Return to the saucepan to heat through. Season the soup with the low-sodium salt and freshly ground black pepper. Stir in the fresh parsley.

⓪ Substitute 600 ml (1 pint) skimmed milk for some of the vegetable stock

Ⓓ
HEALTH STATISTICS
Leeks are rich in fibre and the green part in particular provides folate, vitamin E, iron, betacarotene and vitamin C. They also contain antioxidants that help to protect the body from cancer and heart disease.

SWEET CORN AND BUTTER BEAN CHOWDER WITH GREEN CHILLI CORN BREAD

MAKES 4 SERVINGS

CHOWDER:
2 TABLESPOONS (30 ML) EXTRA VIRGIN OLIVE OIL
1 ONION, CHOPPED
1 CLOVE GARLIC, CRUSHED
2 POTATOES, PEELED AND DICED
600 ML (1 PINT) VEGETABLE STOCK
600 ML (1 PINT) SKIMMED MILK
420 G (14 OZ) TINNED SWEET CORN, DRAINED
420 G (14 OZ) TINNED BUTTER BEANS, DRAINED
FRESHLY GROUND BLACK PEPPER

CORN BREAD:
175 G (6 OZ) CORN MEAL
1 TABLESPOON (15 ML) BAKING POWDER
1/2 TEASPOON (2.5 ML) LOW-SODIUM SALT
2 EGGS
2 TABLESPOONS (30 ML) RAPESEED OR SUNFLOWER OIL
250 ML (9 FL OZ) SOYA MILK OR YOGHURT
1–2 CANNED OR PICKLED CHILLIES, CHOPPED (ACCORDING TO YOUR TASTE)

Preheat the oven to 180ºC/350ºF/Gas mark 4.

First make the corn bread. Mix together the corn meal, baking powder and salt in a large bowl. In a separate bowl combine the eggs, oil and soya milk.

Add the wet mixture to the corn meal mixture and mix together. Add the chopped chillies and pour into a lightly oiled 20cm x 20cm baking dish.

Bake for 25 minutes or until the corn bread is coming away from the sides of the dish and it is risen and golden.

While the corn bread is baking, make the chowder.

Heat the olive oil in a large pan. Add the onion and garlic and cook over a moderate heat for 5 minutes.

Add the potatoes and the stock. Bring to the boil, reduce the heat then simmer for 10 minutes. Add the remaining ingredients and simmer for a further 10 minutes, stirring occasionally. Season with freshly ground pepper to taste.

Serve piping hot with the corn bread.

M

HEALTH STATISTICS
This dish provides a perfect balance of protein (from the beans and milk) and complex carbohydrate (from the sweet corn and corn meal). It is rich in fibre, iron and calcium.

PUMPKIN SOUP

MAKES 4 SERVINGS

1 TABLESPOON (15 ML) EXTRA VIRGIN OLIVE OIL
1 ONION, CHOPPED
2.5 CM (1 IN) PIECE FRESH GINGER, PEELED AND GRATED
1 GARLIC CLOVE, CRUSHED
1/2 TEASPOON (2.5 ML) GRATED NUTMEG
1/2 TEASPOON (2.5 ML) GROUND CORIANDER
1 CARROT, SLICED
1 MEDIUM POTATO, PEELED AND CHOPPED
700 G (11/2 LB) PUMPKIN FLESH, CHOPPED
600 ML (1 PINT) VEGETABLE STOCK
A LITTLE LOW-SODIUM SALT AND FRESHLY GROUND BLACK PEPPER

Heat the olive oil in a large saucepan, add the onion and sauté over moderate heat for about 5 minutes until it is translucent. Add the ginger, garlic, nutmeg and coriander and cook for a further minute.

Add the prepared vegetables, stir well, cover and continue cooking gently for a further 5 minutes. Add the stock, bring to the boil, reduce the heat and simmer for about 20 minutes or until the vegetables are tender.

Liquidise the soup using a hand blender or conventional blender. Add a little more water or stock if you want a thinner consistency. Season to taste with the low-sodium salt and pepper.

Serve the pumpkin soup with a swirl of Greek yoghurt or crème fraîche.

HEALTH STATISTICS
Pumpkin is super-rich in the phytonutrient, alphacarotene, which helps prevent cancer. It is also rich in vitamin E, betacarotene and vitamin C. Both alpha and betacarotene can be converted in the body to vitamin A.

SPICY PARSNIP SOUP

MAKES 4 SERVINGS
2 TABLESPOONS (30 ML) EXTRA VIRGIN OLIVE OIL
1 ONION, FINELY CHOPPED
1 TEASPOON (5 ML) GROUND CUMIN
1 TEASPOON (5 ML) GROUND CORIANDER
225 G (8 OZ) (APPROX 2) PARSNIPS, PEELED AND SLICED
150 G (5 OZ) SWEDE, PEELED AND ROUGHLY CHOPPED
125 G (4 OZ) TURNIP, PEELED AND ROUGHLY CHOPPED
1 LITRE (1³/₄ PINTS) VEGETABLE STOCK
A LITTLE FRESHLY GRATED NUTMEG
A LITTLE LOW-SODIUM SALT AND FRESHLY GROUND BLACK PEPPER

Heat the olive oil in a heavy-based saucepan over a moderate heat. Add the onion and sauté gently for about 5 minutes until it is translucent. Stir in the spices and continue cooking for 1 minute, stirring continuously.

Add the prepared vegetables and stir to coat in oil. Continue cooking gently over a moderately low heat for 5 minutes in a covered pan until the vegetables soften a little.

Add the stock and bring to the boil. Simmer for about 15 minutes or until the vegetables are tender.

Allow the soup to cool a little. Liquidise the soup using a hand blender, food processor or blender. Season to taste with the nutmeg, low-sodium salt and black pepper.

Stir in 150 ml (5 fl oz) natural bio-yoghurt and heat through, but do not allow the soup to boil.

HEALTH STATISTICS
Parsnips are rich sources of complex carbohydrates – which provide slow-release energy – as well as vitamin E. Parsnips, swede and turnips are all rich in potassium and swede is a good source of vitamin C.

MINESTRONE SOUP

MAKES 4 SERVINGS
1 LITRE (1³/₄ PINTS) VEGETABLE STOCK
1 ONION, CHOPPED
2 GARLIC CLOVES, CRUSHED
2 CARROTS, CHOPPED
1 MEDIUM POTATO, PEELED AND DICED
1 LEEK, TRIMMED AND THINLY SLICED
2 TEASPOONS (10 ML) DRIED BASIL
420 G (14 OZ) TINNED HARICOT, CANNELINI OR FLAGEOLET BEANS
2 SMALL COURGETTES, TRIMMED AND SLICED
125 G (4 OZ) FINE GREEN BEANS
125 G (4OZ) SMALL WHEAT-FREE PASTA SHAPES
400 G (14 OZ) TINNED CHOPPED TOMATOES

Pour the vegetable stock into a large saucepan. Bring to the boil and add the onion, garlic, carrots, potatoes, leeks, basil and haricot beans. Lower the heat, cover and simmer for 15 minutes until the vegetables are tender.

Add the courgettes, green beans, tomatoes and pasta and continue cooking for a further 5 minutes or until the pasta is just cooked (check the cooking instructions on the packet).

Serve the soup hot in individual bowls.

0 **Serve with freshly grated Parmesan cheese**

D

HEALTH STATISTICS
This soup is rich in fibre, potassium, vitamin C (from the tinned tomatoes, leeks and courgettes) and betacarotene (from the carrots). The haricot beans are good sources of protein, complex carbohydrate and soluble fibre.

BUTTERNUT SQUASH SOUP

MAKES 4 SERVINGS
1 MEDIUM BUTTERNUT SQUASH
1 LITRE (1³/₄ PINTS) VEGETABLE STOCK
1 LARGE ONION, CHOPPED
1 SMALL SWEDE, PEELED AND CHOPPED
1 TABLESPOON (15 ML) EXTRA VIRGIN OLIVE OIL
A LITTLE LOW-SODIUM SALT AND FRESHLY GROUND BLACK PEPPER

Peel the butternut squash and cut the flesh into chunks.

Place the vegetable stock, butternut squash, onion and swede in a large saucepan. Bring to the boil, lower the heat, cover and simmer for about 20 minutes until the vegetables are tender.

Remove from the heat and liquidise with the olive oil until smooth using a blender, food processor or a hand blender.

Return to the saucepan to heat through. Season the soup with the low-sodium salt and freshly ground black pepper.

D

HEALTH STATISTICS
Butternut squash is super-rich in alphacarotene and betacarotene, both powerful antioxidants that help combat premature ageing, heart disease and cancer. It's also a useful source of vitamin C.

CHAPTER 8
SALADS

Sensational salads made with the freshest vegetables are full of goodness. Raw, lightly grilled, seasonal – vegetables are terrific sources of vitamins, minerals, fibre, antioxidants and protective phytonutrients. Bring out the flavours with fresh aromatic herbs, delicious dressings, and balsamic vinegar…. healthy eating has never tasted so good.

GRILLED PEPPER SALAD WITH MINT AND BASIL

MAKES 4 SERVINGS

2 RED PEPPERS
2 YELLOW PEPPERS
2 ORANGE PEPPERS
3 TABLESPOONS (45 ML) EXTRA VIRGIN OLIVE OIL
1 SMALL ONION, FINELY SLICED LENGTHWAYS
GRATED ZEST AND JUICE OF 1 LEMON
HANDFUL OF FRESH MINT, ROUGHLY TORN
HANDFUL OF FRESH BASIL LEAVES, ROUGHLY TORN

Preheat the grill.

Remove the seeds from the peppers and cut them lengthways into wide strips.

Place the vegetables on a baking tray. Drizzle over a little olive oil and turn so that the vegetables are lightly coated in the oil.

Grill the vegetables for around 3 minutes on each side. Set aside to cool.

Place them in a shallow dish. Add the remaining olive oil, onion, lemon zest and juice, mint and basil and mix well. Mix in the onion slices.

Accompany with a green-leaf salad.

O Use as a tasty filling for wholemeal baps and sandwiches.

HEALTH STATISTICS
Peppers are super-rich in vitamin C and the phytochemicals betacryptoxanthin and betacarotene. All are powerful antioxidants that help protect against heart disease. The vitamin C content of this salad boosts immunity and helps to ward off viral infections.

CHICKEN AND MUSHROOM SALAD WITH A SPICY SESAME DRESSING

MAKES 4 SERVINGS

125 G (4 OZ) PACK READY-WASHED SALAD LEAVES
1 CUCUMBER, SLICED DIAGONALLY
A SMALL HANDFUL OF CHOPPED FRESH MINT
4 SKINLESS BONELESS CHICKEN BREASTS
12 SHITAKE MUSHROOMS

DRESSING:
125 ML (4 FL OZ) RICE VINEGAR
1 TABLESPOON (15 ML) DIJON MUSTARD
4 TABLESPOONS (60 ML) RAPESEED OIL
2 TABLESPOONS (30 ML) SESAME OIL
2 TEASPOONS (10 ML) SOY SAUCE
4 SPRING ONIONS, CHOPPED

To make the dressing: Whisk the vinegar and mustard in a bowl. Gradually whisk in both oils, then the soy sauce. Mix in the spring onions.

Place the chicken and mushrooms in a large glass baking dish. Pour half the dressing over and turn to coat. Cover and chill for at least 30 minutes.

Preheat the grill. Remove chicken and mushrooms from marinade and cook under the grill until cooked through, about 4 minutes per side for the chicken, about 2 minutes per side for the mushrooms. Slice the cooked chicken and halve the mushrooms.

Combine the salad leaves, cucumbers and mint in large bowl. Pour enough dressing over salad to coat and toss gently. Transfer to large plate and spoon the chicken slices and mushrooms on top.

M

HEALTH STATISTICS
Chicken is high in protein and low in fat. It also provides B-vitamins. The shitake mushrooms contain compounds that help fight different cancers and stimulate the immune system.

CARROT, CORIANDER AND CASHEW SALAD

MAKES 4 SERVINGS
85 G (3 OZ) CASHEWS
4 MEDIUM-SIZED CARROTS
JUICE OF HALF A LEMON
4 TABLESPOONS (60 ML) FRESH CORIANDER LEAVES, CHOPPED
FRESHLY GROUND BLACK PEPPER

Lightly toast the cashews by placing under a hot grill or in a preheated oven for a few minutes until pale golden in colour.
Set aside to cool.

Peel and grate the carrots. Transfer to a mixing bowl, add lemon juice, and stir well. Add the cashews and chopped coriander leaves. Toss well and season to taste with the black pepper.

Add 2–3 tablespoons (30–45 ml) plain yoghurt and combine well before serving

D

HEALTH STATISTICS
Carrots are excellent detoxifiers, helping to cleanse the body. They are the richest sources of betacarotene, a powerful anticancer nutrient – one serving of this salad will give you the daily requirement – and they also promote healthy skin and vision. Cashew nuts are rich in heart-healthy monounsaturated oils, zinc, iron and protein.

APPLE WITH CELERY

MAKES 4 SERVINGS
4 CELERY STICKS
2 CRISP RED APPLES

DRESSING:
2 TABLESPOONS (30 ML) EXTRA VIRGIN OLIVE OIL
1 TABLESPOON (15 ML) WALNUT OIL
1 TABLESPOON (15 ML) LEMON JUICE
2 TABLESPOONS (30 ML) CHOPPED FRESH PARSLEY

Slice the celery diagonally. Slice the apples thinly.

Place the extra virgin olive oil, walnut oil and lemon juice in a bottle or screw-top jar and shake together thoroughly.

In a bowl, toss together the celery, apple, dressing, and parsley.

You may substitute 3 tablespoons (45 ml) mayonnaise or natural yoghurt for the dressing.

D

HEALTH STATISTICS
Celery contains a phytonutrient, apigenin, which has antioxidant properties and may benefit high blood pressure and blood cholesterol. It is a good source of potassium, which can also help control blood pressure. This salad is rich in fibre and heart-healthy monounsaturated oils.

COURGETTE SALAD WITH BASIL AND PINE NUTS

MAKES 4 SERVINGS
4 COURGETTES
2 TABLESPOONS (30 ML) EXTRA VIRGIN OLIVE OIL
1 GARLIC CLOVE, SLICED
JUICE OF HALF A LEMON
SMALL HANDFUL OF SULTANAS
SMALL HANDFUL OF PINE NUTS
FRESHLY GROUND BLACK PEPPER

Trim then cut the courgettes into thick slices lengthways. Heat the olive oil in a frying pan. Add the courgettes in a single layer and sauté over medium-high heat for about 2 minutes until the underside is lightly flecked with brown.

Turn carefully, then add the garlic and pine nuts and sauté for another minute, taking care not to let the garlic and pine nuts burn. Lower the heat and cook for a further 5 minutes until the courgettes are just tender.

Transfer to a shallow serving dish. Add the lemon juice, sultanas and pine nuts and season with black pepper.

Serve warm or chilled.

HEALTH STATISTICS
Courgettes contain potassium, betacarotene and vitamin C. Pine nuts are rich in monounsaturated oils and super-rich vitamin E, both of which are excellent heart-protective nutrients. They are also great for the skin and warding off premature wrinkles.

SUMMER SALAD WITH CUMIN AND LIME DRESSING

MAKES 4 SERVINGS

1 LARGE ROMAINE (COS) LETTUCE, TOUGH OUTER LEAVES REMOVED

2 RED PEPPERS, DESEEDED AND DICED

2 CARROTS, GRATED

1 SMALL CUCUMBER, SLICED

4 TOMATOES, QUARTERED

4 SPRING ONIONS, SLICED

A HANDFUL OF VARIOUS HERB LEAVES, E.G. BASIL, FLAT-LEAF PARSLEY, MINT

2 RIPE AVOCADOS

2 TABLESPOONS (30 ML) LIME OR LEMON JUICE

DRESSING:

2 TABLESPOONS (30 ML) LIME JUICE

$1/2$ TEASPOON (2.5 ML) GROUND CUMIN

1 GARLIC CLOVE, CRUSHED

$1/2$ TEASPOON HOT PEPPER SAUCE

4 TABLESPOONS (60 ML) EXTRA VIRGIN OLIVE OIL

FRESHLY GROUND BLACK PEPPER, TO TASTE

Cut the lettuce leaves into $1/2$-inch pieces and place them in a large bowl. Add the peppers, carrots, cucumber, tomatoes and spring onions.

Halve, peel and pit the avocados. Cut them into $1/4$-inch dice and place in a small bowl. Add the lime or lemon juice and toss well (to prevent discolouration). Add the avocados to the other vegetables.

Place the dressing ingredients in a bottle or screw-top glass jar and shake together. Pour over the salad and toss well.

D

HEALTH STATISTICS

This salad is high in fibre and potassium. The romaine lettuce – particularly the darker green outer leaves – contains more betacarotene and iron than most other lettuce varieties. Avocados are rich in vitamin E and heart-healthy monounsaturated oils.

GREEK SALAD WITH FENNEL AND MINT

MAKES 4 SERVINGS
1 ROMAINE (COS) LETTUCE
1 SMALL BULB OF FENNEL
1 CUCUMBER
2 LARGE TOMATOES
1 GREEN, RED OR ORANGE PEPPER
1 RED ONION
115 G (4 OZ) BLACK KALAMATA OLIVES
175 G (6 OZ) FETA CHEESE

DRESSING:
4 TABLESPOONS (60 ML) EXTRA VIRGIN OLIVE OIL
JUICE OF 1 LEMON
A SMALL BUNCH OF FLAT-LEAF PARSLEY, CHOPPED
A LITTLE LOW-SODIUM SALT AND FRESHLY GROUND BLACK PEPPER, TO TASTE

Cut the lettuce into wide ribbons. Halve and thinly slice the fennel, discarding the tough inner 'core'. Cut the cucumber lengthways in half then half again, and then slice thickly. Cut the tomatoes into quarters. Remove the seeds from the pepper and slice it thinly. Slice the onion thinly.

Put the prepared vegetables into a large bowl. Add the feta cheese and olives.

Whisk the dressing ingredients together in a small bowl. Pour the dressing over the salad and toss well.

M

HEALTH STATISTICS
This salad is rich in potassium and vitamin C. The dark green leaves of the romaine lettuce provides betacarotene and iron and the peppers and tomatoes are super-rich in vitamin C. Feta cheese – which is made from sheep or goat's milk – contains 20% fat, which is considerably lower than other hard cheeses (around 30%). It is also rich in calcium and protein, albeit a little lower than Cheddar.

RED KIDNEY BEANS WITH SWEET CORN AND TOMATOES

MAKES 4 SERVINGS

400 G (14 OZ) TINNED RED KIDNEY BEANS, DRAINED AND RINSED

300 G (10 OZ) TINNED (DRAINED AND RINSED) OR THAWED FROZEN SWEET CORN

250 G (9 OZ) CHERRY TOMATOES, HALVED

4 SPRING ONIONS, CHOPPED

A SMALL HANDFUL OF FRESH CORIANDER, CHOPPED

DRESSING:

2 TABLESPOONS (30 ML) EXTRA VIRGIN OLIVE OIL

2 TABLESPOONS (30 ML) LEMON JUICE (1–2 LEMONS)

A LITTLE LOW-SODIUM SALT AND FRESHLY GROUND BLACK PEPPER

In a large bowl, combine the red kidney beans with the sweetcorn, tomatoes, spring onion, and the chopped coriander.

In a small bowl whisk together the olive oil, lemon juice and low-sodium salt. Pour the dressing over the vegetables. Serve the salad at room temperature or chilled slightly.

D

HEALTH STATISTICS
This salad contains a good balance of protein (from the beans) and carbohydrate (from the beans and sweetcorn). Red kidney beans are also rich in soluble fibre – the kind that's good for regulating blood sugar and cholesterol levels – iron and B-vitamins. Sweet corn contains fibre as well as protective antioxidants.

GRILLED SALMON WITH NICOISE SALAD

MAKES 4 SERVINGS

3 EGGS

125 G (4 OZ) FINE GREEN BEANS, TRIMMED AND HALVED

2 'LITTLE GEM' LETTUCES

1 RED ONION, THINLY SLICED

225 G (8 OZ) CHERRY TOMATOES, HALVED

4 TABLESPOONS (60 ML) BLACK OLIVES

4 X 125 G (4 OZ) SALMON STEAKS

1 LEMON, SLICED INTO WEDGES

DRESSING:

3 TABLESPOONS (45 ML) EXTRA VIRGIN OLIVE OIL

1 TABLESPOON (15 ML) LEMON JUICE

$1/2$ TEASPOON (2.5 ML) DIJON MUSTARD

1 SMALL CLOVE OF GARLIC, CRUSHED

Place the eggs in a saucepan of cold water. Bring to the boil and cook for 5 minutes. Drain and plunge into cold water, then peel.

Steam or boil the green beans for 2 minutes. Drain.

Tear the lettuce into bite-sized pieces and place in a bowl with the onions, tomatoes, olives and green beans.

Heat the grill. Brush the salmon steaks with a little olive oil then cook under the grill for about 2–3 minutes each side.

Toss the salad with the dressing. Divide into 4 bowls. Place a salmon steak on top of each. Slice the eggs into quarters and arrange next to the salmon with the lemon wedges.

M

HEALTH STATISTICS

Salmon is an excellent source of the essential omega-3 fatty acids, vital for controlling blood pressure, balancing hormones and promoting healthy skin. This dish is rich in protein, lycopene – a powerful anticancer phytonutrient – and vitamin C.

TUNA AND BABY SPINACH SALAD

MAKES 4 SERVINGS

3 PEPPERS, 1 OF EACH COLOUR (RED, YELLOW AND GREEN), THINLY SLICED

2 TABLESPOONS (30 ML) CHOPPED FRESH PARSLEY LEAVES

HALF A RED ONION, THINLY SLICED

12 LARGE BLACK OLIVES, PITTED

200 G (7 OZ) TUNA IN SPRING WATER, DRAINED AND COARSELY MASHED WITH A FORK

1 PACK (185 G) READY-WASHED BABY SPINACH

DRESSING:

2 TABLESPOONS (30 ML) LEMON JUICE

3 TABLESPOONS (45 ML) EXTRA VIRGIN OLIVE OIL

A LITTLE LOW-SODIUM SALT, TO TASTE

To make the dressing: whisk together the lemon juice, olive oil, and salt in a small bowl.

Combine the peppers, parsley, onion, olives and tuna in a medium-size bowl. Pour the dressing over the salad and toss to coat.

Divide the spinach leaves among 4 plates. Top with the tuna salad. Serve immediately.

M

HEALTH STATISTICS
This salad is high in protein. The peppers are super-rich in vitamin C, a great immunity-booster, and the spinach provides plenty of folic acid, iron and beta-carotene.

COLESLAW WITH HAZELNUTS AND YOGHURT DRESSING

MAKES 4 SERVINGS

1 SMALL WHITE CABBAGE, SHREDDED
4 MEDIUM CARROTS, GRATED
1 RED ONION, THINLY SLICED
30 G (1 OZ) CHOPPED ROAST HAZELNUTS

DRESSING:
4 TABLESPOONS (60 ML) NATURAL BIO-YOGHURT
2 TEASPOONS (10 ML) DIJON MUSTARD
2 TEASPOONS (10 ML) LOW-FAT MAYONNAISE
2 TEASPOONS (10 ML) LEMON JUICE

In a large bowl whisk together the yoghurt, mustard, mayonnaise and lemon juice.

Add the cabbage, carrots, red onion and hazelnuts, tossing to combine well.

HEALTH STATISTICS

Cabbage is rich in fibre, vitamin C and cancer-protective nutrients called glucosinolates. It also helps the liver to detoxify. Carrots are also good 'cleansers' and are super-rich in betacarotene, a powerful antioxidant that helps fight cancer.

HUMMUS

MAKES 4 SERVINGS

400 G (14 OZ) TINNED CHICKPEAS
2 GARLIC CLOVES, CRUSHED
2 TABLESPOONS (30 ML) EXTRA VIRGIN OLIVE OIL
120 ML (4 FL OZ) TAHINI (SESAME SEED PASTE)
JUICE OF 1 LEMON
2–4 TABLESPOONS (30–60 ML) WATER
A LITTLE LOW-SODIUM SALT AND FRESHLY GROUND BLACK PEPPER
A PINCH OF PAPRIKA OR CAYENNE PEPPER

Drain and rinse the chickpeas. Put them in a food processor or blender with the remaining ingredients, apart from the paprika. Process to a smooth paste.

Add extra water if necessary to give the desired consistency. Adjust the seasoning to taste.

Spoon into a serving dish. Pour over a little olive oil and sprinkle with cayenne or paprika. Chill in the fridge for at least 2 hours before serving.

HEALTH STATISTICS

This dip is an excellent source of fibre, protein and iron. Chickpeas also contain fructo-oligosaccharides, a type of fibre that increases the friendly bacteria of the gut and boosts the immune system. Sesame seeds are rich in calcium and magnesium.

MANGO AND AVOCADO SALSA

1 RIPE MANGO
1 AVOCADO
HALF A RED ONION
A SMALL HANDFUL OF FRESH CORIANDER, CHOPPED
1 RED CHILLI, FINELY CHOPPED (OPTIONAL)
1 GARLIC CLOVE, CRUSHED
JUICE OF 2 LIMES
JUICE OF HALF A LEMON
A LITTLE LOW-SODIUM SALT

Slice through the mango either side of the stone. Peel, then cut the flesh into cubes. Halve, peel and chop the avocado. Finely chop the red onion and toss together with the mango and avocado.

Add the coriander, chilli, garlic, lime and lemon juice. Season with the low-sodium salt if necessary.

HEALTH STATISTICS
Mangos are terrific sources of beta-carotene, a powerful antioxidant that helps combat free radicals and is also good for the skin. Avocados are rich in heart-healthy monounsaturated fats and vitamin E; the fresh coriander, lemon and lime juice all provide excellent amounts of vitamin C.

GUACAMOLE (AVOCADO DIP)

MAKES 4 SERVINGS
2 RIPE AVOCADOS
2 TABLESPOONS (30 ML) LEMON OR LIME JUICE
HALF A SMALL RED ONION, FINELY CHOPPED
1 GARLIC CLOVE, CRUSHED
2 MEDIUM TOMATOES, SKINNED AND CHOPPED
1 FRESH GREEN CHILLI, DESEEDED AND CHOPPED (OPTIONAL)
2 TABLESPOONS (30 ML) FRESH CORIANDER, FINELY CHOPPED
SEA SALT AND FRESHLY GROUND BLACK PEPPER
CORIANDER SPRIGS TO SERVE

Halve each avocado; remove the stone and scoop out the flesh. Mash the avocado flesh with the lemon or lime juice, using a fork.

Add the remaining ingredients, mixing well. Check the seasoning, adding a little more black pepper or lemon juice if necessary.

Spoon into a serving dish, cover and chill. Garnish with the coriander sprigs before serving.

HEALTH STATISTICS
Avocado is super-rich in heart-healthy monounsaturated oils, vitamin E, folic acid and potassium. The tomatoes add vitamin C and the antioxidant, lycopene.

CHICKPEA AND RED PEPPER SALAD WITH WALNUTS

MAKES 4 SERVINGS

400 G (14 OZ) TIN CHICKPEAS, DRAINED AND RINSED
1 RED ONION, THINLY SLICED
1 RED PEPPER, DESEEDED AND SLICED
12 BLACK OLIVES, PITTED
1 PACKET (100 G) OF READY-WASHED WATERCRESS
85 G (3 OZ) WALNUTS, LIGHTLY TOASTED

DRESSING:
3 TABLESPOONS (45 ML) EXTRA VIRGIN OLIVE OIL
2 TABLESPOONS (30 ML) BALSAMIC VINEGAR
1 GARLIC CLOVE, CRUSHED
1 TEASPOON (5 ML) DIJON MUSTARD

In a large bowl, mix together the chickpeas, onion, pepper and olives.

Place the dressing ingredients in a bottle or screw-top glass jar and shake until combined. Add half of the dressing to the chickpea salad and mix until well combined.

Toss the watercress with the remaining dressing. Transfer to a serving plate. Top with the chickpea salad and sprinkle with the toasted walnuts.

D

HEALTH STATISTICS
Chickpeas are an excellent source of fibre, protein and iron. Watercress is also rich in iron as well as vitamin C, betacarotene and folate.

ASPARAGUS AND AVOCADO SALAD

MAKES 4 SERVINGS
225 G (8 OZ) ASPARAGUS SPEARS
2 AVOCADOS
2 TABLESPOONS (30 ML) LEMON JUICE
2 TABLESPOONS (30 ML) SESAME SEEDS, LIGHTLY TOASTED

DRESSING:
1 TEASPOON (5 ML) WHOLEGRAIN MUSTARD
1 TEASPOON (5 ML) HONEY
2 TABLESPOONS (30 ML) BALSAMIC VINEGAR

Trim the asparagus spears. Steam for 3 minutes. They should still be quite crunchy. Drain and allow them to cool.

Cut the avocados in half, remove the stone and peel. Dice the flesh and toss immediately in the lemon juice to prevent it from going brown.

Remove the avocado from the lemon juice and mix with the asparagus spears and sesame seeds.

Mix the dressing ingredients in a small bowl, and then drizzle over the salad. Toss well then serve.

D

HEALTH STATISTICS
Asparagus is rich in folate and vitamin E and contains a special type of fibre – fructo-oligosaccharide – that benefits your digestive system. Avocados are excellent sources of monounsaturated oils that help to keep your heart healthy and also do wonders for your skin.

ROCKET, TUNA AND WHITE BEAN SALAD

MAKES 4 SERVINGS
125 G (4 OZ) READY-WASHED ROCKET
4 PLUM TOMATOES, QUARTERED
400 G (14 OZ) TINNED HARICOT OR CANNELINI BEANS, DRAINED AND RINSED
200 G (7 OZ) TIN OF TUNA IN SPRING WATER, DRAINED
4 SPRING ONIONS, CHOPPED INTO 2.5 CM (1 IN) LENGTHS
A HANDFUL OF FRESH PARSLEY, CHOPPED

DRESSING:
2 TABLESPOONS (30 ML) EXTRA VIRGIN OLIVE OIL
1 TABLESPOON (15 ML) LEMON JUICE
1 CLOVE OF GARLIC, FINELY CHOPPED

Place the rocket and tomatoes in a large bowl and mix together. Stir in the beans and the tuna, roughly breaking the tuna up into large flakes. Add the spring onions and parsley.

Shake the olive oil, lemon juice and garlic in a bottle or screw-top glass jar then drizzle over the salad. Toss well and serve.

M

HEALTH STATISTICS
This salad is a good source of protein (from the tuna and beans). The beans are also rich in fibre, magnesium, zinc and iron, while the rocket provides vitamin C, iron and folate.

SWEET CORN AND AVOCADO SALSA

MAKES ABOUT 450 ML (3/4 PINT)
200 G (7 OZ) SWEET CORN KERNELS
1 TABLESPOON (15 ML) FINELY DICED RED ONION
HALF A RED PEPPER, DESEEDED AND FINELY DICED
1 LARGE TOMATO, SKINNED, DESEEDED AND FINELY DICED
A SMALL HANDFUL OF FRESH CORIANDER, FINELY CHOPPED
A LITTLE LOW-SODIUM SALT (OPTIONAL) AND FRESHLY GROUND BLACK PEPPER TO TASTE
1 RIPE AVOCADO, HALVED, PEELED AND DICED
3 TABLESPOONS (45 ML) LIME OR LEMON JUICE

Mix together the sweet corn, onion, red pepper, tomato, fresh coriander, low-sodium salt (if using) and black pepper.

Add the avocado and lime or lemon juice and combine carefully. Check the seasoning, adding a little more lime juice, low-sodium salt or black pepper if necessary.

Chill in the fridge before serving.

D

HEALTH STATISTICS
Sweet corn is rich in the antioxidant zeaxanthin, which helps fight free radicals in the retina. They are also rich in fibre and folic acid. Avocados are super-rich sources of heart-healthy monounsaturated oils as well as vitamin E, folic acid and potassium.

CHAPTER 9
SNACKS

For most people, snacks mean crisps, biscuits, chocolate, cakes … foods that are high in saturated fat, sugar and salt. Even cereal and breakfast cereal bars marketed as healthy alternatives to traditional snacks can be loaded with hydrogenated (processed) artery-clogging fats that overburden your detoxifying systems. The following recipes will provide you with plenty of inspiring ideas for tasty snacks and mini-bites that are easy to make and fit into the detox lifestyle. I have included a selection of savoury and sweet recipes to suit your mood. Many of these are great energy-boosters when you need to eat on the go. Others are equally good served to guests as canapés with drinks.

AVOCADO AND RED PEPPER CROSTINI

MAKES 8

4 THIN SLICES OF RYE BREAD
OLIVE OIL FOR BRUSHING
1 SMALL RIPE AVOCADO, PEELED AND STONED
1 GARLIC CLOVE, CRUSHED
1/2 TEASPOON GROUND CUMIN
JUICE OF HALF A LIME
A LITTLE LOW-SODIUM SALT AND FRESHLY GROUND BLACK PEPPER
8 SMALL THIN STRIPS OF RED PEPPER

To make the crostini, preheat the oven to 180°C/350°F/Gas mark 4.

Cut each bread slice in half diagonally and place them on an oiled baking sheet. Brush each slice lightly with olive oil. Bake in the oven for about 10 minutes until crisp.

Meanwhile, mash the avocado with a fork until smooth. Add the crushed garlic, cumin, lime juice, low-sodium salt and black pepper.

Once the crostini have cooled, spread a spoonful of avocado purée on each slice. Place a red pepper strip on top and serve immediately.

This simple nutritious snack can also be enjoyed with a salad for lunch, or even served with cocktails to guests in the evening.

D

HEALTH STATISTICS
Avocados are rich in monounsaturated fats and vitamin E, both of which help keep the circulatory system in good health and protect the heart. Red peppers are rich in vitamin C and other powerful cancer-protective antioxidants.

ROASTED NUTS

MAKES 200 G (7 OZ)

200 G (7 OZ) WHOLE NUTS, E.G. BLANCHED ALMONDS,
BRAZIL NUTS, CASHEWS, PECAN NUTS
2 TABLESPOONS (30 ML) OLIVE OIL
1/4 TEASPOON (1.25 ML) CAYENNE PEPPER
1 TEASPOON (5 ML) PAPRIKA
1 TABLESPOON (15 ML) SESAME SEEDS

Preheat the oven to 200°C/400°F/Gas mark 6.

Spread the nuts out on a baking sheet and toast in the oven for
5 minutes until they are a pale golden colour.

Lower the temperature to 150°C/300°F/Gas mark 2.

Combine the olive oil, pepper, paprika and sesame seeds in a bowl.
Add the toasted nuts and stir to coat evenly.

Return the mixture to the baking sheet and cook in the oven for
a further 20 minutes, stirring every 5 minutes.

Leave the nuts to cool on the baking sheet. Serve straight away
or store in an airtight container for up to one week.

HEALTH STATISTICS
All nuts are good sources of
protein, vitamin E (which helps
protect against heart disease),
zinc, magnesium, iron and B
vitamins. Although they are rich
in fat, it is the heart-healthy
monounsaturated kind, which
helps lower blood cholesterol
levels. In this recipe, they are
seasoned with spices and
sesame seeds instead of salt.

CELERY WITH CHEESE AND SEEDS

MAKES 1 SERVING
1 TABLESPOON (15 ML) LOW-FAT SOFT CHEESE
1 TEASPOON SUNFLOWER SEEDS, SESAME SEEDS OR PUMPKIN SEEDS
2 STICKS OF CELERY

Combine the soft cheese with the seeds. Spread it into the celery
sticks then cut into 2.5-cm (1-inch) lengths.

This easy savoury snack can also be served to guests instead
of crisps and salted nibbles.

M

HEALTH STATISTICS
Celery is rich in potassium, which
works with sodium to regulate
blood pressure and keep the
kidneys functioning properly.
It is also a natural mild diuretic,
helping reduce water retention.

GRILLED COURGETTES IN A LEMON MARINADE

MAKES 2 SERVINGS
2 COURGETTES
2 TABLESPOONS (30 ML) OLIVE OIL
2 TABLESPOONS (30 ML) LEMON JUICE
FRESHLY GROUND BLACK PEPPER
A FEW FRESH BASIL LEAVES (OPTIONAL)

Trim and cut the courgettes into slices lengthways. Brush both sides of each slice with olive oil and place them on a lightly oiled baking tray. Place under a hot grill for 2–3 minutes. Alternatively, cook briefly in a ridged griddle pan until you have brown stripes on the underside. Place in a shallow dish.

Mix the remaining olive oil, lemon juice, and black pepper in a small bowl. Pour over the courgettes, cover and allow to marinate for at least 2 hours. Scatter over the basil leaves just before serving.

D

HEALTH STATISTICS
Courgettes are rich in potassium, which helps regulate fluid levels in the body. They also supply good amounts of vitamin C and folate. Lemon juice is an excellent source of vitamin C, which helps the body fight infection.

SPICED PINEAPPLE SALSA

MAKES 4 SERVINGS
1 MEDIUM FRESH PINEAPPLE, FINELY DICED
1/2 SMALL RED ONION, FINELY CHOPPED
2.5-CM (1-INCH) PIECE FRESH GINGER, PEELED AND GRATED
1/2 TEASPOON (2.5 ML) GROUND CUMIN
1/2 TEASPOON (2.5 ML) GARAM MASALA
1 TABLESPOON CHOPPED MINT OR CORIANDER LEAVES

Place the pineapple, onion, ginger, spices and mint or coriander in a bowl. Toss gently, cover, and then leave for about 30 minutes for the flavours to blend.

Serve at room temperature.

This tangy salsa tastes great with celery sticks, rice crackers or rye crispbreads.

D

HEALTH STATISTICS
Pineapples are believed to aid digestion because they contain the enzyme bromelain. Raw pineapple is also rich in vitamin C and potassium. Fresh ginger is a good circulatory booster and its anti-inflammatory properties can help alleviate rheumatoid arthritis.

CUCUMBER AND TOMATO RAITA

This refreshing low-fat Indian dish, traditionally served as an accompaniment to curry, can also be served as a dip for vegetable crudités.

MAKES 300 ML (½ PINT)

200 ML (7 FL OZ) NATURAL YOGHURT
½ SMALL ONION, FINELY CHOPPED
7.5-CM (3-INCH) PIECE OF CUCUMBER, SEEDED AND CHOPPED
1 TOMATO, FINELY DICED
1 TEASPOON (5 ML) CUMIN SEEDS, ROASTED AND GROUND*
1 TABLESPOON (15 ML) FRESH CORIANDER, CHOPPED
SQUEEZE OF LEMON OR LIME JUICE

Place the yoghurt in a bowl. Add the onions, cucumber, tomato and cumin seeds. Stir to combine.

Cover and leave in the fridge until required.

Serve garnished with the chopped coriander.

* To roast cumin seeds, place them on a baking sheet and roast in a preheated oven at 200°C/400°F/Gas mark 6 for 5 minutes. Crush coarsely using a pestle and mortar.

HEALTH STATISTICS

Natural yoghurt provides protein and bone-strengthening calcium as well as riboflavin (a B vitamin that helps release energy from carbohydrates). Cucumber is rich in potassium, which helps to regulate fluid balance and alleviate water retention.

TOMATO SALSA

MAKES 4 SERVINGS

2 LARGE RIPE TOMATOES
½ SMALL RED ONION, FINELY CHOPPED
1 CELERY STICK, FINELY CHOPPED
SMALL HANDFUL FRESH CORIANDER, CHOPPED
1 SMALL CLOVE OF GARLIC, CRUSHED
1 TABLESPOON (15 ML) OLIVE OIL
2 TABLESPOONS (30 ML) LEMON OR LIME JUICE

Finely chop the tomatoes and combine in a bowl with the red onion, celery, coriander, garlic, olive oil and lemon or lime juice.

Chill in the fridge before serving.

Top baked potatoes or sweet potatoes with this tangy tomato salsa or simply pile on top of rye crackers, thinly sliced rye bread or cornbread (see recipe page 71)

HEALTH STATISTICS

Tomatoes contain the antioxidant lycopene, which helps protect against prostate cancer and other cancers of the digestive tract. It is also linked to a reduced risk of heart attack and is a useful source of vitamins C and E.

RED PEPPERS FILLED WITH SUNFLOWER AND PUMPKIN SEEDS

MAKES 4 SERVINGS

60 G (2 OZ) MIXTURE OF PUMPKIN AND SUNFLOWER SEEDS
1 CARROT, PEELED AND ROUGHLY CHOPPED
2 TABLESPOONS (30 ML) FRESH PARSLEY
2 TABLESPOONS (30 ML) FRESH BASIL
1 GARLIC CLOVE
1/2 SMALL ONION
2 TABLESPOONS (30 ML) TAHINI*
2 SMALL RED PEPPERS

Put the seeds, carrot, herbs, garlic, and onion in a food processor and process until well blended. Add the tahini and process again until you have a thick purée.

Cut the peppers in half lengthways and remove the seeds and stalk (or you may leave it on for decoration, if you prefer). Fill the peppers with the seed mixture and serve.

*Sesame seed paste is available from health food stores.

D

HEALTH STATISTICS
Red peppers are packed with vitamin C and the phytochemicals betacryptoxanthin and beta-carotene, which help combat the harmful effects of free radicals and improve the health of the skin. Pumpkin seeds are rich in omega-3 oils, which lower your risk of heart disease.

TAHINI DIP

MAKES APPROX 300 ML (½ PINT)
250 ML TAHINI *
1 GARLIC CLOVE, CRUSHED
JUICE OF HALF A LEMON
APPROX 4 TABLESPOONS (60 ML) WATER

Place all the ingredients in a bowl and blend with a hand blender or a small whisk. Adjust the consistency by adding some extra lemon juice or water.

This easy dip is excellent with vegetable crudités, or as a spread for crackers.

*Sesame seed paste is available from health food stores.

HEALTH STATISTICS
Tahini paste, which is made from sesame seeds, is rich in calcium and protein. Although fairly high in fat, it is the healthy unsaturated kind, which helps lower blood cholesterol levels.

BANANA AND WALNUT LOAF

100 ML (3½ FL OZ) SUNFLOWER OIL
2 EGGS
60 ML (2 FL OZ) SOYA, ALMOND, OAT, RICE OR SESAME MILK
225 G (8 OZ) WHEAT-FREE FLOUR
1 TABLESPOON (15 ML) BAKING POWDER (PREFERABLY WHEAT-FREE)
3 LARGE RIPE BANANAS
85G (3 OZ) WALNUTS, CHOPPED

Preheat the oven to 180ºC/350ºF/Gas mark 4. Lightly oil a 500-g (1-lb) loaf tin.

In a large mixing bowl, beat the oil, eggs and milk until light and fluffy.

Fold in the flour and baking powder.

Mash the bananas then add to the mixture with the walnuts. Spoon the mixture into the prepared loaf tin and bake for 1–1¼ hours until a skewer comes out clean.

Turn the loaf out on to a wire rack and leave to cool.

HEALTH STATISTICS
Bananas are a good source of vitamin B6, which the body needs to make the brain chemical serotonin. This feel-good chemical helps to calm the body and regulate appetite. Walnuts are one of the few plant foods naturally rich in alpha-linoleic acid, which helps lower blood cholesterol and improves the elasticity of the skin.

TOFU SESAME SNACKS

MAKES 2 SERVINGS

125 G FAIRLY FIRM TOFU, DRAINED AND CUT INTO BITE-SIZED CUBES
1–2 TABLESPOONS (15–30 ML) SWEET CHILLI SAUCE
2–3 TABLESPOONS (30–45 ML) SESAME SEEDS
SMALL LIME OR LEMON WEDGES

Preheat the grill and line the grill rack with tin-foil.

Put the sweet chilli sauce in a bowl and the sesame seeds on a plate.

Spear each tofu cube with a cocktail stick and dip them into the chilli sauce. Roll in the sesame seeds until well coated.

Arrange the cubes on the lined grill rack and grill the tofu for 2 minutes, or until heated through. Turn frequently during cooking to avoid burning.

Garnish with lime or lemon wedges.

M

HEALTH STATISTICS
Tofu is a great low-fat source of protein. It is also rich in bone-strengthening calcium and contains isoflavones, which help protect against heart disease, certain cancers and menopausal symptoms. Sesame seeds are also rich in calcium as well as iron and zinc.

CORNBREAD

MAKES 8 SLICES

175 G (6 OZ) FINE CORNMEAL
1 TABLESPOON (15 ML) WHEAT-FREE BAKING POWDER
A LITTLE LOW-SODIUM SALT AND FRESHLY GROUND BLACK PEPPER
1 EGG
2 TABLESPOONS (30 ML) OLIVE OIL
250 ML (8 FL OZ) SOYA, ALMOND, OAT, RICE OR SESAME MILK

Preheat the oven to 170°C/325°F/Gas mark 3.

Lightly oil a 500-g (1-lb) loaf tin.

Mix together the cornmeal, baking powder, low-sodium salt and pepper in a large bowl.

In a separate bowl combine the egg, oil and milk. Slowly add this mixture to the dry ingredients, mixing well until the mixture is smooth.

Pour the mixture into the prepared loaf tin and bake for 25–30 minutes until an inserted skewer comes out clean. Turn the loaf out on to a wire rack and leave to cool.

M

HEALTH STATISTICS
This quick and easy bread is a tasty substitute for ordinary bread. It's made with cornmeal, which has a slightly higher fibre content compared to ordinary white (wheat) flour. It's delicious simply spread with a little olive oil margarine or topped with chopped tomatoes mixed with fresh basil and black pepper.

BRAZIL AND ALMOND FLAPJACKS

MAKES 12 FLAPJACKS
150 G (5 OZ) OLIVE OIL MARGARINE
5 TABLESPOONS HONEY
200 G (7 OZ) PORRIDGE OATS
25 G (1 OZ) SUNFLOWER SEEDS
125 G (4 OZ) BRAZIL NUTS, ROUGHLY CHOPPED
60 G (2 OZ) FLAKED ALMONDS

Preheat the oven to 180°C/350°F/Gas mark 4.

Lightly oil a 23-cm (9-inch) square baking tin.

Put the margarine and honey in a heavy-based saucepan and heat together, stirring occasionally, until the margarine has melted. Remove from the heat.

Mix in the oats, sunflower seeds, brazils and almonds until thoroughly combined.

Transfer the mixture into the prepared tin, level the surface and bake in the oven for 20- 25 minutes until golden brown around the edges but still soft in the middle.

Leave in the tin to cool. While still warm, score into 12 bars with a sharp knife.

HEALTH STATISTICS
Brazil nuts are super-rich sources of the heart-protective antioxidant selenium. Just two nuts provide your daily selenium needs. In this recipe, they are combined with almonds and sunflower seeds, which provide calcium and protein. Porridge oats are rich in soluble fibre and iron.

APRICOT AND OAT BARS

MAKES 15 BARS
1 X 250G PACK TOFU, DRAINED
200 ML (7 FL OZ) SUNFLOWER OIL
6 TABLESPOONS HONEY
200G (7 OZ) READY-TO-EAT DRIED APRICOTS, ROUGHLY CHOPPED
400G (14 OZ) PORRIDGE OATS

Preheat the oven to 190ºC/375ºF/Gas mark 5.

Lightly oil an 18 x 25-cm (7 x 10-inch) shallow baking tin.

Place the tofu, oil and honey in a large mixing bowl. Beat thoroughly until smooth. Alternatively, use a food processor and blend for 2 minutes.

Add the apricots and oats and mix thoroughly.

Press the mixture firmly into the prepared tin. Lightly mark the surface into 15 squares then bake in the preheated oven for 25 minutes or until golden brown.

Remove from oven, leave to cool in the tin. When cold cut into the marked squares. Store in an airtight tin.

D

HEALTH STATISTICS
Dried apricots are one of the best natural sources of beta-carotene, the plant form of vitamin A and a powerful antioxidant that helps reduce the risk of heart disease and cancer. They are also rich in soluble fibre, which helps to control blood pressure. Tofu, which is made from soya beans, is high in protein, calcium and isoflavones, which help protect against heart disease, certain cancers and menopausal symptoms.

APRICOT BALLS

MAKES ABOUT 25
125 G (4 OZ) READY-TO-EAT DRIED APRICOTS
125 G (4 OZ) RAISINS
125 G (4 OZ) GROUND ALMONDS

Place the dried apricots and raisins in a food processor, or grinder, and process until they form a very thick purée. Then add the almonds and process again until everything is thoroughly mixed. Add a few drops of water to hold it together, if necessary.

Remove the blades from the food processor and then take walnut-sized amounts of the mixture and roll between the palms of your hands to form balls.

Store in the fridge.

D

HEALTH STATISTICS
These nutritious 'sweets' made from dried fruit and nuts are high in iron, fibre and beta-carotene. Almonds also supply vitamin E, calcium, and protein.

VEGETABLE CRISPS

SELECTION OF VEGETABLES, E.G.
BEETROOT
SWEET POTATO
PARSNIP
CARROTS
OLIVE OIL FOR BRUSHING

Preheat the oven to 200°C/400°F/Gas mark 6.

Peel the vegetables, then cut them into very thin slices, no more than 2 mm thick.

Brush both sides of each vegetable slice lightly with oil and arrange them in a single layer on lightly-oiled baking trays.

Bake the vegetable slices in the oven for about 10 minutes until golden brown. Transfer them on to kitchen paper to absorb any excess oil and leave to cool.

These crisps are ideal for dipping into hummus, guacamole and other dips.

HEALTH STATISTICS
A super-healthy alternative to bought potato crisps, these vegetable crisps are packed with vitamins and minerals and are salt-free. During cooking, the natural sugar content of the vegetables becomes more concentrated (as moisture is lost), so the flavours intensify.

DATE AND WALNUT SWEETS

MAKES ABOUT 25
125 G (4 OZ) WALNUTS
125 G (4 OZ) READY-TO-EAT DRIED DATES
125 G (4 OZ) READY-TO-EAT DRIED FIGS
PINCH EACH OF GROUND CINNAMON AND GRATED NUTMEG

Place the walnuts, dried fruit and spices in a food processor, or grinder, and process until it forms an homogeneous mass. Add a few drops of water if necessary to hold it together.

Remove the blades from the food processor and then take walnut-sized amounts of the mixture and roll between the palms of your hands to form balls.

Store in the fridge.

HEALTH STATISTICS
Walnuts are rich in the essential fatty acid alpha-linoleic acid, which is important for regulating hormones and improving the texture of the skin. Dates are high in soluble fibre, which can help relieve constipation and reduce blood cholesterol levels. They are also rich in potassium, which helps maintain the body's fluid balance and regulate blood pressure.

BLUEBERRY MUFFINS

MAKES 12 MUFFINS

100 ML (3¹/₂ FL OZ) RAPESEED OR SUNFLOWER OIL

125 ML (4 FL OZ) CLEAR HONEY

200 ML (7 FL OZ) SOYA, ALMOND, OAT, RICE OR SESAME MILK

1 EGG

175 G (6 OZ) WHEAT-FREE FLOUR *

125G (4 OZ) FINE CORNMEAL

1-TABLESPOON (15 ML) BAKING POWDER (PREFERABLY WHEAT-FREE)

150 G (5 OZ) FRESH OR FROZEN BLUEBERRIES

Preheat the oven to 200°C/400°F/Gas mark 6.

Line a 12-hole muffin tin with paper cases.

Mix together the oil, honey, milk and egg in a large jug. Sift the flour, cornmeal and baking powder into a bowl. Add the liquid mixture to the dry ingredients and stir until combined (it will be quite runny).

Gently fold in the blueberries.

Spoon the mixture into the muffin tin and bake in the oven for 20 minutes, or until risen and golden. Leave to cool for five minutes, then transfer to a wire rack.

* Available from most supermarkets. Most brands contain rice flour and potato starch.

M

HEALTH STATISTICS

Blueberries have the highest antioxidant ability of all fresh fruit. They contain powerful antioxidants called anthocyanins, which help strengthen capillary walls and combat free radical damage. They are also good sources of immunity-boosting vitamin C.

CHAPTER 10
PASTA, RICE AND GRAINS

Pasta is a mainstay in most people's diets so a recipe book without this delicious food would be unimaginable. I prefer to use pasta made from corn, rice or millet instead of the ordinary wheat variety. It's nutritious, quicker to cook and even tastier. Here, pasta and other healthy grains – rice, millet, soba noodles and couscous – are combined with fresh vegetables, delicious sauces, nuts and pulses to give you plenty of inspiration for main meals.

CREOLE RICE WITH TUNA

MAKES 4 SERVINGS
2 TABLESPOONS (30 ML) EXTRA VIRGIN OLIVE OIL
1 ONION, CHOPPED
**3 PEPPERS (ONE OF EACH COLOUR – RED, YELLOW, GREEN),
DESEEDED AND DICED**
HALF A CHILLI PEPPER, FINELY CHOPPED (OPTIONAL)
3 LARGE TOMATOES, SKINNED, CHOPPED AND DESEEDED
225 G (8 OZ) LONG-GRAIN RICE
600 ML (1 PINT) VEGETABLE STOCK
1 TEASPOON (5 ML) FRESH CHIVES, CHOPPED
1 TEASPOON (5 ML) FRESH PARSLEY, CHOPPED
**A LITTLE LOW-SODIUM SALT AND FRESHLY GROUND BLACK PEPPER,
TO TASTE**
200 G (7 OZ) TINNED TUNA IN WATER, DRAINED

Heat the olive oil in a heavy-based pan. Add the chopped onion and peppers and cook over a moderate heat for about 5 minutes until the vegetables are just softened.

Stir in the chilli (if using), tomatoes and rice. Stir for 1–2 minutes until the rice is shiny and coated in oil. Add the vegetable stock, bring to the boil then simmer for 25 minutes or until the rice is cooked.

Stir in the chives and parsley and season to taste with salt and pepper.

Crumble the tuna into the rice mixture and heat through for a few minutes. Serve.

HEALTH STATISTICS
Wholegrain (brown) rice – unlike the white variety – provides fibre, magnesium, phosphorus, thiamin (vitamin B1) and iron. Peppers are rich in vitamin C and other antioxidants while tuna is rich in protein and B-vitamins.

CHICKEN AND RED PEPPER RISOTTO WITH SPINACH

MAKES 4 SERVINGS
1 TABLESPOON (15 ML) EXTRA VIRGIN OLIVE OIL
1 ONION, CHOPPED
1 RED PEPPER, DESEEDED AND DICED
300 G (10 OZ) ARBORIO (RISOTTO) RICE
1.2 LITRES (2 PINTS) HOT CHICKEN OR VEGETABLE STOCK
125 G (4 OZ) COOKED CHICKEN, CHOPPED
125 G (4 OZ) BABY SPINACH LEAVES
A LITTLE LOW-SODIUM SALT AND FRESHLY GROUND BLACK PEPPER

Heat the olive oil in a large heavy-based saucepan. Add the onion and red pepper and cook over a moderate heat for about 5 minutes, until the vegetables have softened. Add the rice and continue cooking and stirring for 1–2 minutes, until the rice is translucent and shiny.

Add a ladle of the hot stock to the rice and cook, stirring constantly, over a low heat until the liquid has been absorbed. Continue adding the stock to the rice a little at a time and stirring until the liquid has been absorbed, for about 17 minutes.

When the rice is almost done, add the chicken and the spinach leaves and stir to mix evenly. Allow to heat through for 2–3 minutes, then adjust the seasoning to taste with low-sodium salt and pepper and serve hot.

HEALTH STATISTICS
Both red peppers and spinach are rich in vitamin C, a terrific immunity enhancer and a powerful antioxidant to help protect against cancer. Spinach also provides lots of iron and folate.

PASTA WITH BROCCOLI AND PINE NUTS

MAKES 4 SERVINGS
450 G (1 LB) BROCCOLI
2 TABLESPOONS (30 ML) EXTRA VIRGIN OLIVE OIL
1 ONION, CHOPPED
2 GARLIC CLOVES, CRUSHED
400 G (14 OZ) TINNED CHOPPED TOMATOES
2 TABLESPOONS (30 ML) PINE NUTS
85 G (3 OZ) SULTANAS
350 G (12 OZ) NON-WHEAT PASTA
LOW-SODIUM SALT AND FRESHLY GROUND BLACK PEPPER

Divide the broccoli into florets and briefly cook in a pan of boiling water for 3–4 minutes. Drain well and keep warm.

Heat the olive oil in a pan and cook the onion and garlic for 5 minutes until the onion is soft but not brown. Add the tomatoes and season with low-sodium salt and pepper and simmer for a few minutes. Add the broccoli and sultanas.

Toast the pine nuts in a dry pan for a minute or two until they start to turn golden.

Cook the pasta in a large pan of boiling water according to the directions on the packet. Drain and transfer to a serving dish. Mix with the broccoli mixture and the pine nuts.

Scatter with freshly grated Parmesan.

HEALTH STATISTICS
Broccoli contains a sulphoraphane, a powerful anticancer compound that reduces the risk of cancer of the bowel, stomach, breast and lungs. It's also rich in vitamin C – one serving of this dish provides 100% of your daily vitamin C needs – folate and fibre. Pine nuts are an excellent source of heart-healthy monounsaturated oils and vitamin E.

WINTER RISOTTO WITH BUTTERNUT SQUASH

MAKES 4–6 SERVINGS

3 TABLESPOONS (45 ML) EXTRA VIRGIN OLIVE OIL

1 LARGE ONION, CHOPPED (OR 1 ONION)

1 TEASPOON (5 ML) GROUND CUMIN

1 TEASPOON (5 ML) GROUND CORIANDER

300 G (10 OZ) ARBORIO (RISOTTO) RICE

1 LITRE (1³/₄ PINTS) HOT VEGETABLE STOCK

350 G (12 OZ) BUTTERNUT SQUASH, PEELED, DESEEDED AND CUT INTO 12MM (¹/₂ INCH) PIECES

1 MEDIUM COURGETTE, DICED

125 G (4 OZ) FRESH OR FROZEN PEAS

1 TABLESPOON (15 ML) FRESH CHOPPED PARSLEY

SEA SALT AND BLACK PEPPER

30 G (1 OZ) FLAKED TOASTED ALMONDS

Heat the olive oil in a large pan. Add the onion and cook for 2 minutes until translucent. Stir in the spices and continue cooking for a further minute.

Add the rice and stir with a wooden spoon until the grains are coated with the oil. Add the hot vegetable stock one ladle at a time, stirring, and simmer for about 10 minutes.

Add the butternut squash and courgette and continue cooking for a further 5 minutes.

Add the peas and continue cooking for a further 5 minutes until all the liquid has been absorbed and the rice is tender but firm in the centre. Perfect risotto is creamy but not solid, and the rice should still have a little bite.

Stir in the parsley and season to taste. Spoon the risotto into a serving dish, scatter the almonds over and serve immediately.

D

HEALTH STATISTICS

Butternut squash is super-rich in betacarotene, which has powerful antioxidant properties, helping protect against heart disease and cancer. It also benefits the skin and can be converted into vitamin A in the body. This dish also provides good amounts of vitamin C, folate and vitamin E.

SPAGHETTI WITH COURGETTES AND MANGETOUT

MAKES 4 SERVINGS

350 G (12 OZ) NON-WHEAT SPAGHETTI
1 TABLESPOON (15 ML) EXTRA VIRGIN OLIVE OIL
225 G (8 OZ) MANGETOUT, TRIMMED AND HALVED
3 SMALL COURGETTES, TRIMMED AND SLICED
60 G (2 OZ) GREEN OR BLACK OLIVES
A LITTLE LOW-SODIUM SALT AND FRESHLY GROUND BLACK PEPPER
JUICE OF HALF A LIME
A SMALL HANDFUL OF FRESH FLAT-LEAF PARSLEY OR CORIANDER, CHOPPED

Bring a large pan of water to the boil and cook the spaghetti according to the packet instructions. Drain and set aside.

Heat the olive oil in a heavy-based saucepan and sauté the prepared vegetables for about 5 minutes, stirring from time to time.

Add the olives and cooked spaghetti, combine well and continue cooking for a further 3 minutes to heat through. Season with the low-sodium salt, freshly ground black pepper and lime juice. Serve sprinkled with the chopped fresh herbs.

HEALTH STATISTICS
Mangetout are super-rich in vitamin C; courgettes also supply good amounts of this vitamin, while both vegetables provide betacarotene and potassium. Olives are rich in the heart-healthy monounsaturated fats and vitamin E.

PASTA WITH SPRING VEGETABLES

MAKES 4 SERVINGS

2 TABLESPOONS (30 ML) EXTRA VIRGIN OLIVE OIL
1 GARLIC CLOVE, CRUSHED
3–4 SHALLOTS, CHOPPED
125 G (4 OZ) MANGETOUT, TRIMMED
125 G (4 OZ) ASPARAGUS, TRIMMED AND CUT INTO 5CM (2IN) LENGTHS
125 G (4 OZ) BABY SPINACH LEAVES
350 G (12 OZ) NON-WHEAT PASTA SHAPES
A SMALL HANDFUL OF FRESH MINT LEAVES, CHOPPED
A LITTLE LOW-SODIUM SALT AND FRESHLY GROUND BLACK PEPPER

Heat the olive oil in a pan and cook the garlic and shallots for 3 minutes until they have softened.

Steam or boil the vegetables in a minimal quantity of water for 3–4 minutes until tender-crisp. Drain immediately.

Meanwhile, cook the pasta in boiling water according to the packet instructions. Drain, then combine with the cooked vegetables and shallot mixture.

Add the mint and season with low-sodium salt and pepper. Toss well and serve immediately.

D

HEALTH STATISTICS
The green vegetables in this dish are packed with antioxidants and fibre. Spinach is super-rich in betacarotene as well as providing lots of vitamin C, folate and iron. Mangetout are rich in vitamin C and asparagus is rich in folate and vitamin E.

PASTA WITH RED PEPPER AND TOMATO SAUCE

MAKES 4 SERVINGS
350 G (12 OZ) NON-WHEAT PASTA SHAPES
2 RED PEPPERS, DESEEDED AND ROUGHLY CHOPPED
2–3 GARLIC CLOVES, PEELED
250 G (9 OZ) TINNED CHOPPED TOMATOES
A LITTLE LOW-SODIUM SALT AND FRESHLY GROUND BLACK PEPPER
A FEW FRESH BASIL LEAVES

Bring a large pan of water to the boil and add the pasta. Cook according to the packet instructions. Drain and set aside.

Meanwhile, make the sauce. Place the chopped peppers, garlic and tomatoes in a food processor or blender with the low-sodium salt, black pepper and basil leaves. Blend until smooth, adding a little vegetable stock or water for a thinner consistency.

Stir the pepper and tomato sauce into the cooked pasta and place over a gentle heat until warmed through. Serve.

O **Serve sprinkled with a little grated cheese.**

D
HEALTH STATISTICS
Red peppers are super-rich in vitamin C, betacryptoxanthin and betacarotene, all powerful antioxidants that help protect the body from heart disease and cancer. In this recipe, there is minimal loss of vitamins as the peppers are used raw. Tinned tomatoes contain lycopene, another powerful anticancer nutrient.

SOBA NOODLES WITH STIR-FRIED VEGETABLES

MAKES 4 SERVINGS

225 G (8 OZ) SOBA (BUCKWHEAT) NOODLES

1 TABLESPOON (15 ML) SESAME OIL

2 TABLESPOONS (30 ML) RAPESEED OIL

1 ONION, THINLY SLICED

2 GARLIC CLOVES, CRUSHED

1 LARGE CARROT, CUT INTO MATCHSTICK STRIPS

2 CELERY STALKS, SLICED

225 G (8 OZ) SPRING CABBAGE, SHREDDED

125 G (4 OZ) BEAN SPROUTS

1 TABLESPOON (15 ML) LOW-SODIUM SOY SAUCE

85 G (3 OZ) CASHEW NUTS, TOASTED

Bring a large pan of water to the boil, add the noodles and cook for 2 minutes. Drain and rinse under cold running water. Transfer to a bowl, sprinkle with the sesame oil and stir briefly to coat.

Heat the rapeseed oil in a wok, add the prepared vegetables and stir-fry for 3–5 minutes, stirring frequently. Add the soy sauce, cashews, cooked noodles and combine the ingredients together. Heat through briefly and serve immediately.

D

HEALTH STATISTICS

Soba noodles – made from buckwheat flour, which is gluten-free – provide slow-release carbohydrates as well as magnesium and iron. The dish is rich in fibre. Spring cabbage is rich in vitamin C and folate – especially the green outer leaves – and the cashews supply protein, zinc and fibre.

PASTA SPIRALS WITH RED KIDNEY BEANS

MAKES 4 SERVINGS

1 TABLESPOON (15 ML) EXTRA VIRGIN OLIVE OIL

1 ONION, CHOPPED

2 GARLIC CLOVES, CRUSHED

600 G (1 LB 4 OZ) RIPE TOMATOES, SKINNED, DESEEDED AND CHOPPED, OR 500 G TINNED CHOPPED TOMATOES

2 TABLESPOONS (30 ML) TOMATO PASTE

3 TABLESPOONS (45 ML) CHOPPED FRESH PARSLEY

A LITTLE LOW-SODIUM SALT AND FRESHLY GROUND BLACK PEPPER

350 G (12 OZ) NON-WHEAT PASTA SPIRALS

400 G (14 OZ) TINNED RED KIDNEY BEANS, DRAINED AND RINSED

Heat the olive oil in a heavy-based frying pan. Add the onion and garlic and cook over a low heat for 5 minutes until soft and transparent.

Add the chopped tomatoes and tomato paste. Bring to the boil, reduce the heat and simmer for 15 minutes, stirring occasionally. Stir in the chopped parsley and season with the low-sodium salt and black pepper.

Bring a large pan of water to the boil and cook the pasta spirals according to the packet instructions. Drain.

Add the cooked pasta and red kidney beans to the tomato sauce. Stir and cook for a further 4 minutes to heat through. Serve.

D

HEALTH STATISTICS

The tomato sauce is super-rich in lycopene, a potent antioxidant that fights cancer and heart disease, as well as vitamin C. Red kidney beans provide lots of protein, soluble fibre, zinc and iron, and pasta supplies slow-release carbohydrates.

VEGETABLE HOTPOT WITH PASTA TWISTS

MAKES 4 SERVINGS

250 G (9 OZ) NON-WHEAT PASTA TWISTS
2 TABLESPOONS (30 ML) EXTRA VIRGIN OLIVE OIL
2 GARLIC CLOVES
1 ONION, CHOPPED
2 CARROTS, SLICED
2 COURGETTES, TRIMMED AND SLICED
125 G (4 OZ) BUTTON MUSHROOMS
400 G (14 OZ) TINNED CHOPPED TOMATOES
400 G (14 OZ) TINNED BORLOTTI OR RED KIDNEY BEANS
300 ML (1/2 PINT) VEGETABLE STOCK
1 TABLESPOON (15 ML) CORNFLOUR
A LITTLE LOW-SODIUM SALT AND FRESHLY GROUND BLACK PEPPER

Bring a large pan of water to the boil and cook the pasta twists according to the packet instructions. Drain.

Meanwhile, heat the olive oil in a large saucepan and sauté the garlic and onion for 3 minutes over a moderate heat. Add the carrots and cook for a further 5 minutes.

Add the courgettes and mushrooms and continue cooking for a further 3 minutes, stirring occasionally. Add the remaining ingredients except the pasta. Stir well then add the cooked pasta.

Bring to the boil, cover, reduce the heat and simmer for about 15 minutes until the vegetables are tender.

Mix the cornflour with a little water to make a smooth paste. Stir into the hotpot and cook for a further 2 minutes, stirring continuously, until thickened. Season with a little low-sodium salt and freshly ground black pepper

D

HEALTH STATISTICS
This dish provides an excellent balance of protein and complex carbohydrates, as well as vitamins and minerals. It is rich in soluble fibre, which helps lower blood cholesterol, control blood pressure and balance blood sugar levels.

CHESTNUT AND VEGETABLE BURGERS

MAKES 8 BURGERS
125 G (4 OZ) COUSCOUS
150 ML (5 FL OZ) HOT VEGETABLE STOCK
1 TABLESPOON (15 ML) EXTRA VIRGIN OLIVE OIL
1 ONION, FINELY CHOPPED
2 CARROTS, GRATED
1 COURGETTE, FINELY DICED
200 G (7 OZ) DRIED CHESTNUT PIECES
1 EGG, BEATEN
3 TABLESPOONS (45 ML) CHOPPED CHIVES
A LITTLE LOW-SODIUM SALT AND FRESHLY GROUND BLACK PEPPER
EXTRA OLIVE OIL FOR BRUSHING

Place the couscous in a bowl. Pour over the hot stock and leave to stand for 15 minutes until the stock has been absorbed.

Meanwhile, heat the oil in a frying pan and cook the onion over a moderate heat for 5 minutes. Add the carrot and courgette and continue cooking for 5 minutes. Remove from the heat.

Add the chestnuts, couscous, egg, chives and seasoning. Mix well.

Divide the mixture into 8 and firmly press into burger shapes. Chill until ready to serve.

Heat the grill. Place the burgers on a grill tray, brush with a little olive oil then cook for about 15 minutes, turning carefully halfway through the cooking time.

M

HEALTH STATISTICS
Chestnuts are low in fat and provide potassium, B-vitamins and vitamin E. Couscous supplies complex carbohydrates and the carrots are super-rich in betacarotene, a powerful antioxidant that helps protect against cancer and heart disease.

CHICKEN NOODLE SALAD

MAKES 4 SERVINGS
1 SMALL FREE-RANGE CHICKEN, ABOUT 1.5 KG
3 CM FRESH GINGER, PEELED AND GRATED
1 ONION, HALVED
A LITTLE LOW-SODIUM SALT
225 G (8 OZ) RICE VERMICELLI NOODLES
HALF AN ICEBERG LETTUCE, SHREDDED
HALF A CUCUMBER, CUT INTO MATCHSTICK STRIPS
4 SPRING ONIONS, CHOPPED
4 TABLESPOONS (60 ML) SESAME SEEDS, TOASTED

DRESSING:
60 ML (2 FL OZ) RICE VINEGAR
1 TABLESPOON (15 ML) TAHINI (SESAME PASTE) OR PEANUT BUTTER
2 TABLESPOONS (30 ML) SESAME OIL
2 TEASPOONS (10 ML) SOY SAUCE

Place the chicken in a large saucepan, cover with water, add the ginger, onion and low-sodium salt. Cover and bring to the boil, reduce the heat and simmer for 45 minutes.

Drain the chicken, remove the skin, take the meat off the bones and shred it quite finely. Discard the skin and bones.

Put the noodles in a bowl, cover with boiling water and let them soak for 5 minutes. Drain and rinse under cold running water.

Place the noodles in a large bowl. Combine with the prepared vegetables and chicken.

Combine the dressing ingredients in a small bowl and pour over the chicken salad. Toss to combine and sprinkle with toasted sesame seeds.

HEALTH STATISTICS
This salad is rich in protein and B-vitamins (from the chicken), and the vegetables provide plenty of potassium and fibre. The sesame seeds and sesame paste in the dressing are rich in calcium, magnesium and iron.

PENNE WITH CHICKEN AND MUSHROOMS

MAKE 4 SERVINGS

300 G (10 OZ) NON-WHEAT PENNE PASTA (OR OTHER PASTA SHAPES)

300 G (10 OZ) SKINLESS, BONELESS CHICKEN BREASTS

1 TABLESPOON (15 ML) EXTRA VIRGIN OLIVE OIL

2 GARLIC CLOVES, CRUSHED

1 TABLESPOON (15 ML) CIDER VINEGAR

1 TABLESPOON (15 ML) CHOPPED FRESH TARRAGON

150 G (5 OZ) MUSHROOMS, SLICED

150 G (5 OZ) ASPARAGUS SPEARS

1 TABLESPOON (15 ML) CORNFLOUR

400 ML (14 FL OZ) SKIMMED MILK (OR SOYA, RICE OR OAT MILK)

A LITTLE LOW-SODIUM SALT AND FRESHLY GROUND BLACK PEPPER

Cook the penne pasta according to the packet instructions. Drain.

Slice the chicken into thin strips.

Heat the olive oil in a heavy-based pan. Add the chicken and garlic and cook, stirring, for 5 minutes. Add the vinegar and tarragon.

Stir in the mushrooms and asparagus and cook for a further 2–3 minutes.

In a jug, blend the cornflour with a little of the milk to make a smooth paste. Stir in the remainder of the milk. Gradually add to the chicken mixture over a gentle heat, stirring continuously, until the sauce has thickened.

Add the sauce to the drained pasta. Mix together and serve immediately.

HEALTH STATISTICS

This dish is rich in protein and calcium. Chicken also supplies plenty of B-vitamins and the asparagus is rich in folate – needed for healthy blood cells and preventing heart attacks – and vitamin E.

SPICY MILLET WITH ROASTED HAZELNUTS

MAKES 4 SERVINGS

1 TABLESPOON (15 ML) EXTRA VIRGIN OLIVE OIL

1 ONION, CHOPPED

1 RED PEPPER, DESEEDED AND CHOPPED

1/2 TEASPOON (2.5 ML) CUMIN

1/2 TEASPOON (2.5 ML) TURMERIC

225 G (8 OZ) MILLET

600 ML (1 PINT) VEGETABLE STOCK

225 G (8 OZ) FROZEN PEAS

85 G (3 OZ) HAZELNUTS

JUICE OF 1 LEMON

1 TABLESPOON (15 ML) CHOPPED FRESH MINT

Heat the oil in a large heavy-based pan and cook the onion and red pepper for 5 minutes over a moderate heat. Add the spices and fry for 1 minute, stirring continually.

Add the millet and the vegetable stock, bring to the boil, cover and simmer for 20 minutes, stirring occasionally until the stock has been absorbed and the millet is light and fluffy. Add the peas during the last 5 minutes of the cooking time.

Place the hazelnuts in a frying pan over a high heat for 2–3 minutes until lightly toasted, shaking the pan occasionally.

Stir the nuts, lemon juice and mint into the millet mixture and serve.

O **You can add chopped cooked chicken, prawns or any other vegetable to this millet dish.**

D

HEALTH STATISTICS

Millet is gluten-free and is a rich source of magnesium and iron. This dish is also a good source of vitamin C (from the peppers), vitamin E and monounsaturated oils (both from the hazelnuts).

SPICED LENTILS AND RICE

MAKES 4 SERVINGS
1 TABLESPOON (15 ML) RAPESEED OIL
1 ONION, SLICED
3–4 CARDAMOM PODS
3–4 CLOVES
2–3 CINNAMON STICKS
A LITTLE LOW-SODIUM SALT
1 GARLIC CLOVE, CRUSHED
2 CM (1 IN) FRESH ROOT GINGER, FINELY CHOPPED
150 G (5 OZ) COOKED LENTILS
225 G (8 OZ) BROWN RICE

Heat the oil in a heavy-based saucepan then add the onion, cardamom pods, cloves and cinnamon sticks. Gently fry, stirring now and then, until the onion has turned golden, around 10 minutes. Add the low-sodium salt, garlic and ginger and mix well.

Mix in the cooked lentils, basmati rice and 300 ml of water. Bring to the boil then reduce the heat to very low. Cover the pan and simmer for 15–20 minutes until the water has been absorbed and the rice is tender. Serve.

D

HEALTH STATISTICS
Lentils are an excellent source of protein, B-vitamins, iron, zinc and magnesium. The basmati rice provides slow-release complex carbohydrates.

WHOLEGRAIN RICE PILAF WITH GREEN BEANS AND PINE NUTS

MAKES 4 SERVINGS

2 TABLESPOONS (30 ML) EXTRA VIRGIN OLIVE OIL

1 ONION, FINELY CHOPPED

2 LEEKS, TRIMMED AND FINELY SLICED

2 GARLIC CLOVES, CRUSHED

1 TEASPOON (5 ML) GROUND CORIANDER

300 G (10 OZ) WHOLEGRAIN (BROWN) RICE

900 ML (1 1/2 PINTS) VEGETABLE STOCK

225 G (8 OZ) GREEN BEANS, TRIMMED AND HALVED

60 G (2 OZ) PINE NUTS, TOASTED

A LITTLE LOW-SODIUM SALT AND FRESHLY GROUND BLACK PEPPER

Heat the oil in a large heavy-based pan. Add the onion, leeks and garlic and cook over a moderate heat for 10 minutes until softened but not browned.

Add the coriander and brown rice and cook, stirring, for 1 minute until the grains are glossy. Add the vegetable stock and bring to the boil. Cover and simmer for 20–25 minutes until the liquid has been absorbed and the rice is cooked. Add the green beans during the last 5 minutes of the cooking time.

Stir in the toasted pine nuts and season with the low-sodium salt and pepper. Serve.

D

HEALTH STATISTICS

Wholegrain (brown) rice – unlike the white variety – provides fibre, magnesium, phosphorus, thiamin (vitamin B1) and iron. Leeks and onions are rich in sulphur-containing phytochemicals – allyl sulphides – which are protective against heart disease and cancer. They also provide good amounts of folate and vitamin C. The pine nuts provide protein and are super-rich in heart-healthy vitamin E and monounsaturated oils.

CHAPTER 11
VEGETABLES

Vegetables are terrific cleansers and detoxifiers and a powerhouse of immune-enhancing nutrients. Nothing can be more delicious than simply cooked fresh vegetables. Lightly steamed with pan-fried fish, roasted with rosemary Mediterranean-style, grilled with fresh herbs, filled with ricotta, stir-fried with garlic and spices …. the possibilities are endless.

FLORENTINE JACKETS

MAKES 4 SERVINGS
2 BAKING (LARGE) POTATOES
225 G (8 OZ) PACK OF READY-WASHED SPINACH LEAVES
125 G (4 OZ) RICOTTA CHEESE
A LITTLE LOW-SODIUM SALT AND FRESHLY GROUND BLACK PEPPER
FRESHLY GRATED NUTMEG
3–4 TABLESPOONS (45–60 ML) MILK

Preheat the oven to 200°C/400°F/Gas mark 6.

Scrub the potatoes. Prick with a fork. Place on a baking tray and bake in the oven for 1–1½ hours (depending on the size) until soft when gently pressed.

Place the spinach in a large saucepan with a tablespoon of water. Cover. Wilt over a low heat for a few minutes. Chop roughly and season with the low-sodium salt, black pepper and nutmeg.

Cut the potatoes in halves. Scoop the potato out of the skins and place in a bowl. Mash with the milk.

Mix together the mashed potato, spinach and ricotta cheese.

Spoon the mixture back into the potato skins. Place on the baking sheet and return to the oven for 15 minutes until piping hot.

M
HEALTH STATISTICS
Spinach is an excellent source of iron, betacarotene, folate, vitamin E and vitamin C. It also contains powerful antioxidants such as lutein, which helps to reduce the risk of cancer. Keeping the cooking time short preserves the vitamin C and folate content.

COURGETTE AND TOMATO TIAN

MAKES 4 SERVINGS
2 LARGE COURGETTES
2–3 TABLESPOONS OF FRESH HERBS, E.G. OREGANO, THYME OR ROSEMARY
1 RED PEPPER, DESEEDED AND CUT INTO STRIPS
450 G (1 LB) PLUM TOMATOES
3–4 TABLESPOONS (45–60 ML) EXTRA VIRGIN OLIVE OIL
2 GARLIC CLOVES
FRESHLY GROUND BLACK PEPPER

Preheat the oven to 200°C/400°F/Gas mark 6.

Lightly oil a shallow baking dish.

Slice the courgettes and arrange in an overlapping layer in the bottom of the dish. Sprinkle with half of the herbs.

Arrange a layer of peppers then a layer of tomato wedges. Sprinkle with the remaining herbs and the black pepper.

Mix the garlic and olive oil in a small jug, and then pour over the vegetables. Cover the dish with foil.

Bake for about 45 minutes, removing the foil during the last 10 minutes of cooking time.

Serve with cooked wholegrain rice or quinoa.

Ⓞ **Serve with crusty bread and goat's cheese.**

Ⓓ
HEALTH STATISTICS
This dish is super-rich in vitamin C (from the tomatoes and red pepper), betacarotene and lycopene (both from the tomatoes), a powerful antioxidant that helps to protect against heart disease and cancers of the stomach, colon and prostate. The fresh herbs are super-rich in calcium, magnesium, iron and vitamin E.

SPICY CHICKPEAS WITH TOMATOES AND COURGETTES

MAKES 4 SERVINGS
2 TABLESPOONS (30 ML) RAPESEED OIL
1 ONION, CHOPPED
2 GARLIC CLOVES, CRUSHED
1 CM PIECE FRESH GINGER, PEELED AND FINELY GRATED
1 GREEN CHILLI, FINELY CHOPPED
1 TEASPOON (5 ML) GROUND CORIANDER
1 TEASPOON (5 ML) GROUND CUMIN
¼ TEASPOON (1.25 ML) TURMERIC
400 G (14 OZ) TINNED CHOPPED TOMATOES
2 X 400 G (14 OZ) TINS CHICKPEAS, DRAINED AND RINSED
2 COURGETTES, TRIMMED AND SLICED
125 G (4 OZ) FINE GREEN BEANS, TRIMMED AND HALVED
A LITTLE LOW-SODIUM SALT AND FRESHLY GROUND BLACK PEPPER
A HANDFUL OF FRESH CORIANDER LEAVES, CHOPPED

Heat the oil in a large heavy-based saucepan and add the onions, garlic, ginger, chilli, coriander, cumin and turmeric. Cook over a moderate heat for 10 minutes until the onions have softened.

Add the tomatoes, chickpeas, courgettes and green beans. Bring to the boil, and then simmer for 10 minutes. Season with the low-sodium salt and pepper.

Stir in the fresh coriander just before serving.

Serve with cooked wholegrain rice.

Serve with chapattis or naan bread instead of the rice if you prefer.

HEALTH STATISTICS
Chickpeas are an excellent source of fibre, protein and iron. They also contain fructo-oligosaccharides, a type of fibre that maintains healthy gut flora and increases the friendly bacteria of the gut – especially useful if your gut bacteria get upset by travel or stress.

BABY AUBERGINES WITH COURGETTES AND FRESH TOMATO SAUCE

MAKES 4 SERVINGS

4 BABY AUBERGINES
2 TABLESPOONS (30 ML) EXTRA VIRGIN OLIVE OIL
FRESHLY GROUND BLACK PEPPER
JUICE OF HALF A LEMON

FOR THE FILLING:
1 TABLESPOON (15 ML) OLIVE OIL
1 ONION, FINELY CHOPPED
1 GARLIC CLOVE, CRUSHED
1 LARGE COURGETTE, FINELY CHOPPED
SMALL HANDFUL OF FRESH BASIL LEAVES

FOR THE TOMATO SAUCE:
1 TABLESPOON (15 ML) EXTRA VIRGIN OLIVE OIL
1 ONION, CHOPPED
2 GARLIC CLOVES, CRUSHED
600G (1 LB 4 OZ) RIPE TOMATOES, SKINNED, DESEEDED AND CHOPPED, OR 500G TINNED CHOPPED TOMATOES
2 TABLESPOONS (30 ML) TOMATO PASTE
A LITTLE LOW-SODIUM SALT AND FRESHLY GROUND BLACK PEPPER

Preheat the oven to 190°C/375°F/Gas Mark 5.

Slice off the aubergine tops and halve them lengthways. Cut a crisscross pattern in the flesh and place them cut-side up in a large roasting tray. Brush with 2 tablespoons of olive oil and the juice of half a lemon. Season with freshly ground pepper.

Roast the aubergines in the oven for approximately 20–25 minutes until the flesh is softened.

Meanwhile, make the tomato sauce. Heat the olive oil in a heavy-based frying pan. Add the onion and garlic and cook over a low heat for 5 minutes until soft and transparent. Add the chopped tomatoes and tomato paste. Bring to the boil, reduce the heat and simmer for 15 minutes, stirring occasionally. Season with a little salt and black pepper.

To make the filling, heat the olive oil in a heavy-based frying pan. Add the onion and garlic and fry gently for 5 minutes until softened. Add the chopped courgette and continue cooking for 10 minutes stirring frequently, until the courgette is soft. Mix in the basil leaves.

Spoon the filling mixture over the aubergines in the roasting tray and return to the oven for a few minutes to heat through.

Place the aubergines on a serving plate and spoon over the tomato sauce.

O **Before returning the aubergines to the oven, sprinkle 45 g (1½ oz) fresh breadcrumbs, blended with a little fresh basil and garlic and 25 g (1 oz) freshly grated Parmesan cheese over the courgette filling and bake for 10 minutes until the crumbs are crisp and golden.**

D

HEALTH STATISTICS
Aubergines are rich in potassium and contain the anticancer nutrient, nasuin. The tomato sauce is an excellent source of lycopene, a potent antioxidant that fights cancer and heart disease.

MEXICAN BEAN BAKE WITH A RYE CRUMB TOPPING

MAKES 4 SERVINGS

- 2 TABLESPOONS (30 ML) EXTRA VIRGIN OLIVE OIL
- 1 LARGE RED ONION, CHOPPED
- 2 CLOVES GARLIC, CRUSHED
- 1 RED PEPPER, DESEEDED AND DICED
- 1 GREEN PEPPER, DESEEDED AND DICED
- 1 TEASPOON (5 ML) DRIED BASIL
- 450 ML (1 PINT) PASSATA (SIEVED TOMATOES)
- 1 VEGETABLE STOCK CUBE (LOW-SALT OR SALT-FREE)
- 420 G (14 OZ) TINNED RED KIDNEY BEANS, DRAINED AND RINSED
- 420 G (14 OZ) TINNED PINTO BEANS, DRAINED AND RINSED
- 1 TABLESPOON (15 ML) CHOPPED FRESH PARSLEY
- 60 G (2 OZ) FRESH RYE BREAD CRUMBS

Preheat the oven to 200°C/400°F/Gas mark 6.

Heat the olive oil in a large pan. Add the onion, garlic and peppers and cook over a moderate heat for 5 minutes.

Add the herbs, passata, stock cube and beans. Bring to the boil, stirring, and then simmer for 10–15 minutes. Stir in the fresh parsley.

Spoon the bean mixture into a baking dish then sprinkle over the bread crumbs.

Bake uncovered for 15 minutes until the breadcrumbs are crispy and golden. (Alternatively, heat under a hot grill for 4–5 minutes.)

HEALTH STATISTICS

The beans provide protein as well as carbohydrate, zinc, magnesium and iron. The peppers are super-rich in vitamin C – one serving of this dish will meet your daily requirement for this vitamin – and the passata is rich in the cancer-protective phytonutrient, lycopene.

SPICY BUTTER BEANS WITH SWEET POTATOES

MAKES 4 SERVINGS

2 MEDIUM SWEET POTATOES (WEIGHING ABOUT 300 G/ 10 OZ EACH), PEELED AND DICED

2 TABLESPOONS (30 ML) EXTRA VIRGIN OLIVE OIL

1 ONION, CHOPPED

2 CLOVES GARLIC, CRUSHED

1¹/₂ TEASPOONS (7.5 ML) MEDIUM CURRY PASTE (OR ACCORDING TO TASTE)

400 G (14 OZ) TINNED CHOPPED TOMATOES

85 G (3 OZ) BUTTON MUSHROOMS, HALVED

420 G TINNED BUTTER BEANS, DRAINED

1 TABLESPOON (15 ML) EACH CHOPPED FRESH CORIANDER AND MINT

Cook the sweet potatoes in a steamer or in boiling water for 5 minutes until they are just soft but firm. Drain.

Heat the olive oil in a large pan. Add the onion and garlic and fry for 5 minutes.

Add the curry paste and cook, stirring continuously for 1 minute. Add the tomatoes, mushrooms, chickpeas and the sweet potatoes. Bring to the boil then simmer for 10 minutes.

Just before serving, stir in the chopped fresh herbs. Transfer to a serving dish.

 Just before serving, stir in 150 ml (¹/₄ pint) natural yoghurt along with the herbs.

D

HEALTH STATISTICS

Sweet potatoes are excellent sources of betacarotene, a potent anticancer nutrient. They also contain vitamins C and E, which, together with betacarotene, fight harmful free radicals. Butter beans provide protein, iron and fibre.

COUSCOUS WITH ROASTED PEPPERS, TOMATOES AND MINT

MAKES 4 SERVINGS
2 TABLESPOONS (30 ML) EXTRA VIRGIN OLIVE OIL
1 SMALL RED PEPPER
1 SMALL YELLOW PEPPER
200 G (7 OZ) CHERRY TOMATOES, HALVED
225 G (8 OZ) COUSCOUS
300 ML (1/2 PINT) HOT VEGETABLE STOCK OR WATER
400 G (14 OZ) TIN RED KIDNEY BEANS, DRAINED AND RINSED
A SMALL HANDFUL OF FRESH MINT, CHOPPED
A LITTLE LOW-SODIUM SALT AND FRESHLY GROUND BLACK PEPPER

Preheat the oven to 200°C/400°F/Gas mark 6.

Remove the seeds from the peppers and cut them into wide strips. Place in a large roasting tin with the cherry tomatoes, drizzle over the olive oil and toss lightly so that the vegetables are well coated in the oil. Roast in the oven for about 30 minutes until the peppers are slightly charred on the outside and tender in the middle. Allow to cool then roughly chop the peppers.

Put the couscous in a large bowl and cover with the hot stock or water. Stir briefly, cover and allow to stand for 5 minutes until the stock has been absorbed. Fluff up with a fork.

Add the roast peppers, tomatoes, beans and mint. Season to taste with the low-sodium salt and black pepper. Serve.

HEALTH STATISTICS
This dish is a rich source of vitamin C (from the peppers) and lycopene, a powerful antioxidant (from the tomatoes) that can fight cancer. The red kidney beans are rich in protein, fibre, zinc and iron.

ROASTED MEDITERRANEAN VEGETABLES WITH PINE NUTS

MAKES 4 SERVINGS

1 AUBERGINE

2 RED PEPPERS

3 COURGETTES

1 RED ONION

3 TABLESPOONS (45 ML) EXTRA VIRGIN OLIVE OIL

2 GARLIC CLOVES, CRUSHED

A FEW SPRIGS OF ROSEMARY

ABOUT 12 BLACK OLIVES

1–2 TABLESPOONS (15–30 ML) PINE NUTS, TOASTED

Preheat the oven to 200°C/400°F/Gas mark 6.

Trim then slice the aubergine and courgettes into wide strips. Remove the seeds from the peppers and cut them into wide strips. Cut the red onion into wedges.

Place the vegetables in a large roasting tin with the garlic and rosemary. Drizzle over the olive oil and toss lightly so that the vegetables are well coated in the oil.

Roast in the oven for about 30 minutes until the vegetables are slightly charred on the outside and tender in the middle. Mix with the black olives.

Serve sprinkled with the toasted pine nuts.

Accompany with 300 ml (10 fl oz) natural yoghurt or thick, Greek-style yoghurt.

HEALTH STATISTICS

Red peppers are super-rich in vitamin C and betacarotene, both powerful antioxidants with anticancer effects. Both the aubergines and courgettes are rich in potassium, which helps to balance fluid levels in the body. Courgettes are also good sources of vitamin C and folate.

GRILLED RED PEPPERS WITH RICOTTA AND BASIL

MAKES 4 SERVINGS

4 LARGE RED PEPPERS
175 G (6 OZ) RICOTTA CHEESE
A LITTLE LOW-SODIUM SALT AND FRESHLY GROUND BLACK PEPPER
A SMALL HANDFUL OF FRESH BASIL LEAVES, CHOPPED
1–2 TABLESPOONS (15–30 ML) EXTRA VIRGIN OLIVE OIL

TOMATO SAUCE:
1 TABLESPOON (15 ML) EXTRA VIRGIN OLIVE OIL
1 ONION, CHOPPED
1 GARLIC CLOVE, CRUSHED
450 G (1 LB) RIPE TOMATOES, SKINNED, DESEEDED AND CHOPPED, OR 400G TINNED CHOPPED TOMATOES
A LITTLE LOW-SODIUM SALT AND FRESHLY GROUND BLACK PEPPER

Preheat the grill.

Brush the peppers with a little of the olive oil, place them in a shallow tin, then place under the grill, turning frequently, until blistered and blackened all over. Put in a bowl, cover with cling film and leave to cool. Carefully remove the skin. Cut each pepper into quarters lengthways, removing the seeds.

Heat the oven to 200°C/400°F/Gas mark 6.

Season the ricotta with low-sodium salt and pepper and mix in the basil. Take a heaped teaspoon of the mixture and place at the narrow end of each pepper. Roll up and place in an ovenproof dish.

Brush each pepper with olive oil and place the dish in the oven for 10 minutes.

Meanwhile, make the tomato sauce. Heat the olive oil in a heavy-based frying pan. Add the onion and garlic and cook over a low heat for 5 minutes until soft and transparent. Add the chopped tomatoes. Bring to the boil, reduce the heat and simmer for 10 minutes, stirring occasionally. Season with a little salt and black pepper. Serve with the grilled peppers.

HEALTH STATISTICS
Red peppers are super-rich in vitamin C, betacryptoxanthin and betacarotene, all powerful antioxidants that help protect the body from heart disease and cancer. Ricotta cheese is relatively low in fat (11%) and provides protein and calcium.

SEA BASS WITH SPRING VEGETABLES

MAKES 4 SERVINGS

4 X 250 G (9 OZ) SEA BASS FILLETS

2 TABLESPOONS (30 ML) EXTRA VIRGIN OLIVE OIL

125 G (4 OZ) FINE GREEN BEANS, TRIMMED AND CUT INTO 5 CM (2 IN) LENGTHS

125 G (4 OZ) SUGAR-SNAP PEAS, TRIMMED

125 G (4 OZ) ASPARAGUS, TRIMMED AND CUT INTO 5 CM (2 IN) LENGTHS

150 G (5 OZ) FRESH OR FROZEN BROAD BEANS

420 G (14 OZ) TINNED FLAGEOLET BEANS, DRAINED AND RINSED

Heat the oven to 180°C/350°F/Gas mark 4.

Pan-fry each sea bass fillet in the olive oil for 1 minute each side to seal, then transfer on to a baking tray and finish cooking in the oven for 8–10 minutes.

Steam or boil the green beans, sugar-snap peas, asparagus and broad beans for 4 minutes until they are tender-crisp. Add the flageolet beans 1 minute before the end of the cooking time so they heat through.

Place the sea bass in the centre of each plate then scatter the vegetables around. Serve immediately.

M

HEALTH STATISTICS

The sea bass is rich in protein and B-vitamins, while the vegetables provide plenty of fibre, potassium and protective antioxidants. Sugar-snap peas are rich in vitamin C, the beans supply protein and iron, and the asparagus is a good source of folate.

BREAST OF CHICKEN WITH BUTTERNUT SQUASH MASH

MAKES 4 SERVINGS

4 CHICKEN BREASTS ON THE BONE
A LITTLE EXTRA VIRGIN OLIVE OIL
4 MEDIUM POTATOES
1 BUTTERNUT SQUASH
6 TABLESPOONS (90 ML) SKIMMED MILK
A LITTLE LOW-SODIUM SALT AND FRESHLY GROUND BLACK PEPPER
A SMALL HANDFUL OF FRESH FLAT-LEAF PARSLEY, CHOPPED

Heat the oven to 190°C/375°F/Gas mark 5.

Scrub and prick the potatoes and cook in the oven for 45–60 minutes, depending on the size of the potatoes.

Meanwhile, place the chicken breasts in a roasting tin, drizzle over a little olive oil; turn the chicken so that they are well coated with oil.

Peel the butternut squash and cut the flesh into large chunks. Place in a separate baking tin, drizzle over a little oil and toss until well coated.

Cook the chicken and the squash in the oven for 20–30 minutes, depending on the size of the chicken breasts. The squash should be soft but not mushy.

Halve the potatoes and scoop out the flesh into a bowl. Add the cooked squash and milk, season with the salt and pepper and mash until smooth. Adjust the consistency with a little extra milk if you wish.

Divide the mash between four plates and place a chicken breast on top. Scatter over the chopped flat-leaf parsley and serve immediately.

M

HEALTH STATISTICS
Butternut squash is super-rich in betacarotene, which has powerful antioxidant properties, helping protect against heart disease and cancer. The potatoes provide complex carbohydrates, fibre and vitamin C. Chicken is rich in protein and B-vitamins.

STIR-FRIED CHICKEN WITH BROCCOLI

MAKES 4 SERVINGS

2 TABLESPOONS (30 ML) EXTRA VIRGIN OLIVE OIL

300 G (10 OZ) CHICKEN BREASTS CUT INTO THIN STRIPS

1 TABLESPOON (15 ML) LIGHT (LOW-SODIUM) SOY SAUCE

1 ONION, THINLY SLICED

2.5 CM (1 IN) PIECE FRESH GINGER, PEELED AND FINELY CHOPPED

225 G (8 OZ) BROCCOLI FLORETS

1 TEASPOON (5 ML) CORNFLOUR BLENDED WITH 1 TABLESPOON (15 ML) WATER

A HANDFUL OF FRESH CHIVES, CHOPPED

Heat the olive oil in a wok, add the chicken and stir-fry for 2–3 minutes until the chicken is lightly browned. Remove from the wok, place on a plate and keep warm.

Add the onion and ginger and stir-fry for 1 minute. Add the broccoli, continue cooking for 3 minutes, then return the chicken to the wok. Pour over the cornflour mixture, stirring continuously, until the mixture thickens.

Serve with cooked rice or noodles.

HEALTH STATISTICS
Chicken provides protein and B-vitamins. Broccoli is rich in sulphoramine, a powerful antioxidant that fights cancer, as well as vitamin C and folate.

CHICKPEAS WITH BUTTERNUT SQUASH AND TOMATOES

MAKES 4 SERVINGS

1 TABLESPOON (15 ML) EXTRA VIRGIN OLIVE OIL

2 ONIONS, CHOPPED

1 RED PEPPER, DESEEDED AND CHOPPED

225 G (8 OZ) BUTTERNUT SQUASH, PEELED AND CHOPPED

400 G (14 OZ) TINNED CHOPPED TOMATOES

250 ML (8 FL OZ) VEGETABLE STOCK

420 G (14 OZ) TINNED CHICKPEAS, DRAINED AND RINSED

Heat the oil in a heavy-based pan, add the onion and pepper and cook over a moderate heat for 5 minutes.

Add the squash, tomatoes, vegetable stock and chickpeas, stir then bring to the boil. Lower the heat and simmer for 20 minutes, stirring occasionally.

Serve with jacket potatoes.

 Serve sprinkled with a little grated cheese

HEALTH STATISTICS
Chickpeas are rich in protein, iron and soluble fibre. They also contain fructo-oligosaccharides, a type of fibre that maintains healthy gut flora and increases the friendly bacteria of the gut.

LENTIL AND VEGETABLE DAHL WITH CASHEW NUTS

MAKES 4 SERVINGS
2 ONIONS, CHOPPED
2 TABLESPOONS (30 ML) RAPESEED OIL
2 GARLIC CLOVES, CRUSHED
1 TEASPOON (5 ML) GROUND CUMIN
2 TEASPOONS (10 ML) GROUND CORIANDER
1 TEASPOON (5 ML) TURMERIC
175 G (6 OZ) RED LENTILS
750 ML (1¼ PINTS) VEGETABLE STOCK
2 CARROTS, DICED
85 G (3 OZ) COURGETTES, SLICED
125 G (4 OZ) FROZEN PEAS
125 G (4 OZ) CASHEW NUTS, TOASTED
1 TABLESPOON (15 ML) LEMON JUICE
A LITTLE LOW-SODIUM SALT
A SMALL HANDFUL OF FRESH CORIANDER, FINELY CHOPPED

Heat the oil in a heavy-based pan and sauté the onions for 5 minutes. Add the garlic and spices and continue cooking for 1 minute while stirring continuously.

Add the lentils, stock, carrots and courgettes. Bring to the boil. Cover and simmer for about 20 minutes, adding the peas 5 minutes before the end of the cooking time.

Stir in the cashew nuts then season with the lemon juice and low-sodium salt. Finally, stir in the fresh coriander.

D **Serve topped with a spoonful of natural yoghurt.**

D
HEALTH STATISTICS
Red lentils are rich in protein, complex carbohydrates and soluble fibre. They provide slow-release energy and help balance blood sugar levels. Red lentils are also rich in iron, zinc and B-vitamins. Cashews supply further protein and zinc.

VEGETABLE CHILLI

MAKES 4 SERVINGS

1 ONION, CHOPPED

1 GREEN PEPPER, CHOPPED

2 CELERY STICKS, SLICED

175 ML (6 FL OZ) WATER

2 GARLIC CLOVES, CRUSHED

400 G (14 OZ) TINNED CHOPPED TOMATOES

1 TABLESPOON (15 ML) TOMATO PASTE

1 VEGETABLE BOUILLON CUBE

1 TABLESPOON (15 ML) CHOPPED FRESH PARSLEY

1–2 TEASPOONS (5–10 ML) CHILLI POWDER, OR TO TASTE

$1/2$ TEASPOON (2.5 ML) GROUND CUMIN

2 X 400 G (2 X 14 OZ) TINS RED KIDNEY BEANS, DRAINED AND RINSED

Combine the onion, pepper, celery, water and garlic in a large saucepan. Cook over a medium-high heat, stirring occasionally, for 6–8 minutes or until the vegetables are tender.

Add the tomatoes, tomato paste, bouillon, parsley, chilli powder and cumin; stir well. Stir in the beans. Bring to the boil, cover, then reduce the heat and simmer, stirring occasionally, for 45 minutes.

Serve with boiled wholegrain rice.

O **Serve topped with a spoonful of natural yoghurt or soured cream.**

D

HEALTH STATISTICS

Red kidney beans are rich in protein, soluble fibre, zinc and iron. They also provide slow-release energy. The vegetables add additional fibre, the peppers are super-rich in vitamin C and the tinned tomatoes are an excellent source of the antioxidant, lycopene.

BEAN PROVENÇALE WITH BLACK OLIVES

MAKES 4 SERVINGS

2 TABLESPOONS (30 ML) EXTRA VIRGIN OLIVE OIL

2 ONIONS, SLICED

1 RED PEPPER, DESEEDED AND SLICED

1 GREEN PEPPER, DESEEDED AND SLICED

2 GARLIC CLOVES, CRUSHED

2 COURGETTES, TRIMMED AND SLICED

400 G (14 OZ) TINNED CHOPPED TOMATOES

420 G (14 OZ) TINNED CANNELINI BEANS OR BUTTER BEANS

2 TABLESPOONS (30 ML) TOMATO PASTE

2 TEASPOONS (10 ML) DRIED OREGANO OR BASIL

60 G (2 OZ) BLACK OLIVES

A LITTLE LOW-SODIUM SALT AND FRESHLY GROUND BLACK PEPPER

A SMALL HANDFUL OF FRESH PARSLEY OR BASIL LEAVES, CHOPPED

Heat the olive oil in a heavy-based pan and sauté the onions and peppers over a moderate heat until soft. Add the garlic and courgettes and continue cooking for a further 5 minutes, stirring occasionally.

Add the tomatoes, beans, tomato paste and dried herbs. Cover and simmer for 15–20 minutes, adding the olives 5 minutes before the end of the cooking time. Season with the low-sodium salt and black pepper. Serve sprinkled with the parsley or basil leaves.

D

HEALTH STATISTICS
Cannelini beans are rich in protein, complex carbohydrate and soluble fibre, which help balance blood sugar and insulin levels. The peppers are super-rich in vitamin C, a powerful antioxidant that helps prevent cancer and heart disease. Olives supply plenty of heart-healthy monounsaturated fats and vitamin E.

FISH STEW WITH FENNEL AND TOMATOES

MAKES 4 SERVINGS
2 TABLESPOONS (30 ML) EXTRA VIRGIN OLIVE OIL
1 FENNEL BULB, FINELY SLICED
1 GARLIC CLOVE, CRUSHED
500 ML (16 FL OZ) FISH OR VEGETABLE STOCK
800 G (18 OZ) TINNED CHOPPED TOMATOES
250 G (9 OZ) CHERRY TOMATOES, HALVED
A LITTLE LOW-SODIUM SALT AND FRESHLY GROUND BLACK PEPPER
450 G (1 LB) MONKFISH FILLET, CUT INTO 4 CM CHUNKS
1 TABLESPOON (15 ML) CHOPPED CHIVES

Heat the olive oil in a large pan, add the fennel and cook over a moderate heat for 5 minutes. Add the garlic and cook for a further minute.

Stir in the stock and tinned tomatoes, bring to the boil and simmer gently for 5 minutes.

Add the cherry tomatoes and cook for a further 5 minutes. Season with low-sodium salt and freshly ground pepper.

Add the monkfish, cover and cook for approximately 5 minutes or until the fish is cooked. Serve the stew in 4 individual bowls and garnish with the chopped chives.

M

HEALTH STATISTICS
This dish is rich in protein and B-vitamins (from the fish). Fennel provides folate and potassium and the tomatoes are rich in vitamin C and lycopene, a powerful antioxidant nutrient that helps fight cancer.

RATATOUILLE WITH RED KIDNEY BEANS

MAKES 4 SERVINGS
2 TABLESPOONS (30 ML) EXTRA VIRGIN OLIVE OIL
1 ONION, CHOPPED
1 EACH OF RED, YELLOW AND GREEN PEPPERS, DESEEDED AND SLICED
2 CLOVES OF GARLIC, CRUSHED
2 COURGETTES, TRIMMED AND SLICED
1 AUBERGINE, DICED
700 G (1 1/2 LB) TOMATOES, SKINNED AND CHOPPED
(OR USE 400 G/ 14 OZ TINNED TOMATOES)
420 G (14 OZ) TINNED RED KIDNEY BEANS, DRAINED
175 G (6 OZ) GREEN BEANS, TRIMMED AND HALVED
A LITTLE LOW-SODIUM SALT AND FRESHLY GROUND BLACK PEPPER
2 TABLESPOONS (30 ML) BASIL LEAVES OR CHOPPED FRESH PARSLEY

Heat the oil in a large saucepan. Add the chopped onion and peppers and cook gently for 5 minutes.

Add the garlic, courgettes, aubergines, tomatoes, red kidney beans and green beans. Stir then cover and cook over a low heat for 20–25 minutes until all the vegetables are tender.

Season to taste with low-sodium salt and freshly ground black pepper and stir in the fresh herbs. Serve hot or cold.

D

HEALTH STATISTICS
This dish is super-rich in antioxidant nutrients: vitamin C (from the peppers and green beans), nasuin (from the aubergine), lycopene (from the tomatoes) and quercetin (from the onions). The red kidney beans provide plenty of soluble fibre, protein and iron.

CHAPTER 12
SHAKES, SMOOTHIES AND JUICES

Making smoothies, shakes and juices is a really easy
way to meet your five a day target for fruit and vegetables.
Packed with vital nutrients, they really do your body, mind
and skin good. Drinks made from fresh ingredients help
energise your body, detox your system, revitalise your
senses and de-stress your mind.

SMOOTHIES

- For best taste and nutritional value, choose ripe fruit.

- Remove thick peel (e.g. from bananas), stones (e.g. from peaches) and hulls (e.g. from strawberries) and cut the flesh into large chunks.

- You may substitute frozen fruit – such as raspberries – for fresh fruit

- If your blender crushes ice, start with ice cubes blended to a 'snow' followed by the fruit. Otherwise, crush the ice before putting it into a blender.

- Add ingredients to the blender beginning with liquids and ending with solids.

- Add more or less juice or water to your smoothie, according to your own preferences, to make a thinner or thicker drink.

MELON AND MINT SMOOTHIE

A CUPFUL OF CRUSHED ICE
1 GENEROUS SLICE HONEYDEW MELON
85 ML (3 FL OZ) GRAPE OR APPLE JUICE
1–2 TEASPOONS (5–10 ML) LEMON JUICE
120 ML (4 FL OZ) NATURAL YOGHURT
1 TABLESPOON (15 ML) CHOPPED MINT LEAVES

Place the ice, melon, fruit juice, lemon juice, yoghurt and mint in a smoothie maker, blender or food processor and process until slushy. Serve immediately.

HEALTH STATISTICS
This refreshing smoothie is rich in potassium, vitamin C, calcium and protein. It has natural diuretic properties, helping reduce water retention.

APRICOT AND MANGO SMOOTHIE

4 APRICOTS, STONES REMOVED
HALF A MANGO, PEELED, STONE REMOVED AND CHOPPED
1 BANANA
150 ML (5 FL OZ) APPLE JUICE
A LARGE CUPFUL OF CRUSHED ICE

Place the ingredients in a smoothie maker, blender or food processor and blend until smooth. Serve immediately.

D

HEALTH STATISTICS

Apricots and mangoes are super-rich in betacarotene, a powerful antioxidant nutrient that helps combat cancer and also benefits the skin. The smoothie also provides fibre, potassium and vitamin B6.

STRAWBERRY AND BANANA SMOOTHIE

MAKES 2 DRINKS
250 ML (8 FL OZ) ORANGE JUICE
125 G (4 OZ) STRAWBERRIES
2 BANANAS, FROZEN AND SLICED *

Place the orange juice, strawberries and frozen banana slices in a smoothie maker, blender or food processor and process until smooth and thick. Serve immediately.

* Use frozen bananas instead of adding ice cubes to the drinks. Peel bananas, place in a plastic bag and freeze.

D

HEALTH STATISTICS

This smoothie is super-rich in vitamin C, potassium, vitamin B6 and fibre.

SUMMER BERRY SMOOTHIE

MAKES 2 DRINKS
A QUARTER OF A MEDIUM CANTALOUPE MELON, PEELED, SEEDED AND CHOPPED
175 G (6 OZ) STRAWBERRIES
175 G (6 OZ) RASPBERRIES
A CUPFUL OF CRUSHED ICE

If you don't mind the small seeds, blend the ingredients together in a smoothie maker, blender or food processor. Alternatively, juice the fruit in a juice extractor; pour into glasses filled with crushed ice and serve immediately.

D

HEALTH STATISTICS
Strawberries and raspberries are rich in immunity-boosting vitamin C, potassium and antioxidants. The cantaloupe melon is an excellent source of betacarotene, a great anticancer nutrient.

ORANGE AND MANGO SMOOTHIE

MAKES 2 DRINKS
1 ORANGE, PEELED AND SEGMENTED
1 MANGO, HALVED, PEELED AND STONE REMOVED
HALF A SMALL PAPAYA, PEELED, SEEDED AND CHOPPED
1 SMALL BANANA, PEELED
CRUSHED ICE

Place the ingredients in a smoothie maker, blender or food processor and blend until smooth. Serve immediately.

D

HEALTH STATISTICS
Oranges and papayas are super-rich in vitamin C, while mangoes and papayas are both rich sources of betacarotene, great for healthy skin and combating harmful free radicals. The banana provides potassium and vitamin B6.

MANGO, MELON AND PEACH SMOOTHIE

MAKES 2 DRINKS

150 ML (5 FL OZ) GRAPE JUICE
150 ML (5 FL OZ) ORANGE JUICE
HALF A MANGO, HALVED, PEELED AND STONE REMOVED
2 SLICES GALIA OR HONEYDEW MELON, PEELED, SEEDED AND CHOPPED
1 PEACH, SKINNED, STONED AND CHOPPED
CRUSHED ICE

Place the ingredients in a smoothie maker, blender or food processor and blend until smooth. Serve immediately.

HEALTH STATISTICS
This smoothie is rich in betacarotene, vitamin C and potassium – all of which will benefit your nails and skin.

BLACKCURRANT AND CRANBERRY SMOOTHIE

MAKES 2 DRINKS

225 G (8 OZ) BLACKCURRANTS
150 ML (5 FL OZ) PURPLE OR RED GRAPE JUICE
150 ML (5 FL OZ) CRANBERRY JUICE DRINK
A CUPFUL OF CRUSHED ICE

If you don't mind the small seeds, place the ingredients in a smoothie maker, blender or food processor and blend until smooth. Alternatively, juice the blackcurrants in a juice extractor then combine with the fruit juices. Pour into ice-filled glasses and serve immediately.

HEALTH STATISTICS
The blackcurrants and purple grape juice are super-rich in vitamin C and powerful antioxidants called anthocyanins, which promote healthy-looking skin and protect against heart disease. Cranberry juice is also vitamin C-rich and helps prevent urinary tract infections.

STRAWBERRY AND PINEAPPLE SMOOTHIE

MAKES 2 DRINKS
125 G (4 OZ) STRAWBERRIES, HULLED
HALF A PEAR, PEELED, CORED AND ROUGHLY CHOPPED
A QUARTER OF A PINEAPPLE, CORED AND CHOPPED
125 ML (4 FL OZ) FRESH ORANGE JUICE
A CUPFUL OF CRUSHED ICE

Place the ingredients in a smoothie maker, blender or food processor and blend until smooth and frothy. Serve immediately.

D

HEALTH STATISTICS
Strawberries and orange juice are both super-rich sources of vitamin C. The pineapple provides fibre and potassium.

RASPBERRY AND PINK GRAPEFRUIT SMOOTHIE

MAKES 2 DRINKS
225 G (8 OZ) RASPBERRIES
300 ML (1/2 PINT) PINK GRAPEFRUIT JUICE
1 BANANA
A LITTLE HONEY, TO TASTE

If you don't mind the small seeds, blend the raspberries, half the grapefruit juice, banana and honey in a smoothie maker, blender or food processor and blend until smooth. Alternatively, juice the fruit in a juice extractor. Add the remaining grapefruit juice, adjusting to your preferred consistency. Serve in chilled glasses immediately.

D

HEALTH STATISTICS
This smoothie is a terrific source of vitamin C and antioxidant nutrients. It is also a great detoxifier, stimulating the function of the liver and digestive system.

STRAWBERRY, LYCHEE AND WATERMELON SMOOTHIE

MAKES 2 DRINKS
A HANDFUL OF CRUSHED ICE
JUICE AND ZEST OF 1 LIME
85 G (3 OZ) STRAWBERRIES
6 FRESH OR CANNED LYCHEES, STONES REMOVED
HALF A MANGO, PEELED AND ROUGHLY CHOPPED
A QUARTER OF A WATERMELON, PEELED AND CHOPPED
1 BANANA, PEELED AND ROUGHLY CHOPPED

Place the ice and fruit in a smoothie maker, blender or food processor and blend until smooth. Serve in chilled glasses immediately.

D

HEALTH STATISTICS
Strawberries and lime juice are super-rich in vitamin C; the mango and watermelon are packed with betacarotene and the watermelon also provides lots of the antioxidant nutrient, lycopene.

PINEAPPLE AND COCONUT SMOOTHIE

HALF A PINEAPPLE
125 ML (4 FL OZ) COCONUT MILK
1 BANANA
150 ML (5 FL OZ) PINEAPPLE JUICE
A CUPFUL OF CRUSHED ICE

Place the ingredients in a smoothie maker, blender or food processor and blend until smooth. Serve immediately.

D

HEALTH STATISTICS
This smoothie is rich in fibre, potassium and vitamin C.

NECTARINE AND BLUEBERRY SMOOTHIE

MAKES 2 DRINKS
2 NECTARINES, HALVED, STONED AND CUT INTO CHUNKS
125 G (4 OZ) BLUEBERRIES
250 ML (9 FL OZ) APPLE JUICE
A CUPFUL OF CRUSHED ICE

Place the prepared fruit, apple juice and ice in a smoothie maker, blender or food processor and blend until smooth. Serve in chilled glasses immediately.

D
HEALTH STATISTICS
Nectarines are rich in betacarotene and vitamin C. Blueberries are super-rich sources of immunity-boosting vitamin C and antioxidants called anthocyanins.

STRAWBERRY AND KIWI FRUIT SMOOTHIE

MAKES 2 DRINKS
A CUPFUL OF CRUSHED ICE
125 G (4 OZ) STRAWBERRIES
1 KIWI FRUIT
1 BANANA
150 ML (5 FL OZ) APPLE JUICE
1 TABLESPOON (15 ML) LINSEEDS (GROUND)

Place the ice, strawberries, kiwi fruit, banana and apple juice in the goblet of a smoothie maker, blender or food processor and process until smooth. Add the ground linseeds and blend until well combined. Serve immediately.

D
HEALTH STATISTICS
Vitamin C-rich summer fruits will boost your energy levels. The linseeds in this drink are rich in heart-healthy omega-3 oils and are, themselves, powerful intestinal cleansers.

JUICES

TOP TIPS

- Wash the fruit and vegetables. Trim them if necessary, stone the fruit and remove any thick peel. Cut them into manageable pieces.

- You can put most parts of the produce into the juicer, except hard skins (e.g. citrus peel, banana peel, etc.) and stones (e.g. from avocados, peaches, apricots, etc.)

- Choose fruit that is ripe yet quite firm. Avoid overripe or very soft fruit as these do not pass through the juice extractor well.

- Drink juices as soon as possible after preparation. Once they are left to stand, they start losing nutrients through oxidation.

- Dilute juices with a little water according to your taste preference.

BLUEBERRY AND BLACKBERRY

MAKES 2 DRINKS

125 G (4 OZ) BLUEBERRIES
2 APPLES CUT INTO QUARTERS
350 G (12 OZ) BLACKBERRIES

Using a juice extractor, juice all the ingredients, pour into a glass and serve immediately.

D

HEALTH STATISTICS
Blueberries and blackberries contain vitamin C as well as powerful antioxidants, which boost immunity and protect the body from illness.

ORANGE, MELON AND NECTARINE

MAKES 2 DRINKS
2 ORANGES
HALF A CANTALOUPE MELON
1 NECTARINE

Using a juice extractor, juice all the ingredients, pour into a glass and serve immediately.

D

HEALTH STATISTICS
This drink is a super immune booster. Oranges, melon and nectarine all provide vitamin C while the cantaloupe melon is rich in betacarotene.

TOMATO AND CELERY

MAKES 2 DRINKS
6 TOMATOES
2 CELERY STICKS
HALF A RED PEPPER

Using a juice extractor, juice all the ingredients, pour into a glass and serve immediately.

D

HEALTH STATISTICS
Tomatoes are super-rich in lycopene, which can help combat several cancers, as well as vitamin C. The red pepper boosts the vitamin C content further and the celery adds to the cleansing properties of this juice

GREENS AND PINEAPPLE

MAKES 2 DRINKS

1 BUNCH OF WATERCRESS
4 BROCCOLI SPEARS
1 BUNCH OF PARSLEY
1 CELERY STICK
HALF A PINEAPPLE

Using a juice extractor, juice all the ingredients, pour into a glass and serve immediately.

D

HEALTH STATISTICS
This juice is super-rich in vitamin C, betacarotene, iron, magnesium, folic acid and calcium. It stimulates detoxification and is also a great immune booster.

CUCUMBER AND MINT

MAKES 2 DRINKS

1 CUCUMBER
1 APPLE
1 PEAR
4 SPRIGS OF FRESH MINT

Using a juice extractor, juice all the ingredients, pour into a glass and serve immediately.

D

HEALTH STATISTICS
This juice is a wonderful cleanser. Cucumber is a good diuretic, helping reduce water retention. This juice provides potassium, vitamin C and antioxidant nutrients.

GRAPE AND CELERY

MAKES 2 DRINKS
225 G (8 OZ) GREEN SEEDLESS GRAPES
4 CELERY STICKS

Using a juice extractor, juice all the ingredients,
pour into a glass and serve immediately.

HEALTH STATISTICS
This cleansing juice also benefits
the skin and immune system. It
provides antioxidant nutrients,
potassium and vitamin C.

CARROT AND PEPPERS

MAKES 2 DRINKS
2 CARROTS
1 RED PEPPER
1 YELLOW PEPPER

Using a juice extractor, juice all the ingredients,
pour into a glass and serve immediately.

HEALTH STATISTICS
Carrots and peppers are super-
rich in betacarotene, a powerful
antioxidant that helps prevent
cancer. Peppers are also highly
concentrated in immunity-
boosting vitamin C.

CARROT, BEETROOT AND CELERY

MAKES 2 DRINKS
2 CARROTS
1 APPLE
HALF AN ORANGE
A QUARTER OF A BEETROOT
2 CELERY STICKS

Using a juice extractor, juice all the ingredients, pour into a glass and serve immediately.

D

HEALTH STATISTICS
This juice has terrific cleansing properties. It is rich in betacarotene, vitamin C, potassium and antioxidant nutrients.

APPLE, CARROT AND GINGER

MAKES 2 DRINKS
3 APPLES
2 CARROTS
1 CM ($1/2$ IN) PIECE FRESH GINGER ROOT

Using a juice extractor, juice all the ingredients, pour into a glass and serve immediately.

D

HEALTH STATISTICS
Apples, carrots and ginger are all good 'cleansers', stimulating the liver and intestines. Carrots are rich in betacarotene, and apples provide the anticancer nutrient, quercetin.

APPLE, ORANGE AND LIME

MAKES 2 DRINKS
3 APPLES
1 ORANGE
HALF A LIME

Using a juice extractor, juice all the ingredients, pour into a glass and serve immediately

D

HEALTH STATISTICS
Apples are good for aiding digestion and provide the antioxidant quercetin and vitamin C, while the orange and lime provide additional vitamin C.

SHAKES

- Keep the fat content low by using skimmed milk or low-fat yoghurt in the recipes

- You may substitute soya milk or yoghurt, oat, rice or almond milk for the dairy version given in the recipes.

- For a thicker shake, add extra fruit (bananas produce the thickest creamiest consistency), crushed ice, or more yoghurt. If you use frozen fruit, the result will be a thicker drink.

- For maximum nutritional value and taste, drink your shake immediately.

BLUEBERRY YOGHURT SHAKE

M

HEALTH STATISTICS
Blueberries are super-rich sources of immunity-boosting vitamin C and antioxidants called anthocyanins. The bio-yoghurt provides protein, calcium and B-vitamins, and the live culture it contains helps promote a healthy gut.

MAKES 2 DRINKS
200 G (7 OZ) BLUEBERRIES
1 SMALL BANANA, PEELED AND SLICED
120 ML (4 FL OZ) APPLE JUICE
150 ML (5 FL OZ) NATURAL BIO-YOGHURT
CRUSHED ICE

Put the blueberries, banana, apple juice, bio-yoghurt and ice into a smoothie maker, blender or food processor and blend until smooth. Serve immediately.

RASPBERRY AND CRANBERRY SHAKE

MAKES 2 DRINKS

A CUPFUL OF CRUSHED ICE
250 ML (8 FL OZ) CRANBERRY AND RASPBERRY JUICE DRINK
125 G (4 OZ) RASPBERRIES
1 CARTON (150 G) NATURAL BIO-YOGHURT

Place the ice, cranberry juice, raspberries and yoghurt in the goblet of a smoothie maker, blender or food processor and process until the ingredients are thoroughly combined. Serve immediately.

HEALTH STATISTICS
Super-rich in vitamin C, this shake also provides powerful antioxidants that help your body fight off viruses and infections. Live yoghurt also boosts your immunity and improves the balance of beneficial bacteria in the gut.

MANGO AND GINGER SHAKE

MAKES 2 DRINKS

1 MANGO, PEELED, STONE REMOVED AND CUT INTO CHUNKS
A HANDFUL OF CRUSHED ICE
2 CM (1 IN) PIECE FRESH ROOT GINGER
250 ML (8 FL OZ) SKIMMED MILK OR NATURAL BIO-YOGHURT

Put the mango flesh, ice, ginger and milk or yoghurt into a smoothie maker, blender or food processor and blend until smooth. Serve immediately.

HEALTH STATISTICS
Mango is rich in betacarotene and vitamin C while the skimmed milk provides plenty of calcium and protein.

BANANA, HONEY AND ALMOND SHAKE

MAKES 2 DRINKS
A CUPFUL OF CRUSHED ICE
300 ML (10 FL OZ) SKIMMED MILK
1 RIPE BANANA
1 TABLESPOON (15 ML) CLEAR HONEY
25 G (1 OZ) GROUND ALMONDS

Place the ice, milk, banana, almonds and honey in the goblet of a smoothie maker, blender or food processor and process until thick and frothy. Drink immediately.

M

HEALTH STATISTICS
This shake drink provides a super balance of protein, carbohydrate and essential fats. Almonds are rich in vitamin E, calcium and protein; the milk also provides protein and calcium while the bananas supply magnesium, potassium and vitamin B6.

BREAKFAST SHAKE

MAKES 2 DRINKS
250 ML (8 FL OZ) OAT, SOYA OR RICE MILK
1 TABLESPOON (15 ML) OAT BRAN
2 TEASPOONS (10 ML) SMOOTH PEANUT BUTTER
JUICE OF HALF A LEMON
A CUPFUL OF CRUSHED ICE
1 BANANA

Place all the ingredients in a smoothie maker, blender or food processor and process until smooth and frothy. Adjust the consistency with milk, if necessary. Serve immediately.

D

HEALTH STATISTICS
This shake provides soluble fibre – from the oat bran – which helps control blood sugar levels, cholesterol levels and even satisfy hunger. It is rich in B-vitamins, protein, calcium, vitamin B6 and potassium.

STRAWBERRY AND NECTARINE SHAKE

MAKES 2 DRINKS

A CUPFUL OF CRUSHED ICE
1 CARTON (150 ML) STRAWBERRY BIO-YOGHURT
6–8 STRAWBERRIES
1 NECTARINE, STONE REMOVED AND ROUGHLY CHOPPED
SKIMMED MILK

Put the ice, yoghurt, strawberries and nectarine in the goblet of a smoothie maker, blender or food processor and process until slushy. Adjust the consistency with skimmed milk. Serve immediately.

M

HEALTH STATISTICS
This nutritious shake is a terrific way of boosting your protein intake. It also provides good amounts of calcium, vitamin C, betacarotene and fibre.

STRAWBERRY BANANA SHAKE

MAKES 2 DRINKS

A CUPFUL OF CRUSHED ICE
125 G (4 OZ) STRAWBERRIES
200 ML (7 FL OZ) SKIMMED MILK
1 BANANA

Put the ice, strawberries, milk and banana in the goblet of a smoothie maker, blender or food processor and process until smooth. Adjust the consistency with milk, if necessary. Serve immediately.

M

HEALTH STATISTICS
Strawberries are super-rich in vitamin C and the banana provides additional fibre and potassium. The milk adds protein and calcium.

CHAPTER 13
DESSERTS

Contrary to popular myth, desserts need not be fattening.
In fact, they can be positively healthy. Here seasonal
fresh fruit, berries, exotic fruit and even dried fruit – rich
in immunity-boosting vitamins and antioxidants – form
the basis of mouth-watering salads, jellies, mousses,
sorbets and crumbles. Enjoy!

ORANGE AND APRICOT SORBET

MAKES 4 SERVINGS
300 ML (¹/₂ PINT) WATER
125 G (4 OZ) SUGAR
3 TABLESPOONS (45 ML) LEMON JUICE
GRATED ZEST AND JUICE OF 1 LARGE ORANGE
400 G (14 OZ) FRESH APRICOTS, HALVED AND STONED
1 EGG WHITE

Put the water, sugar, lemon juice, orange zest and juice into a saucepan and bring to the boil, stirring until the sugar has dissolved. Boil rapidly for about 5 minutes. Add the apricots and simmer gently for 2 minutes. Leave to cool.

Pour the fruit and syrup into a food processor or blender and process to a smooth purée.

Pour into a container suitable for freezing, cover and freeze for about 2 hours until frozen around the sides. Alternatively, pour the mixture into an ice-cream machine and freeze until half-frozen.

Whisk the egg white until it forms soft peaks. If using an ice-cream maker add to the half-frozen mixture and continue freezing until completely frozen. Otherwise, tip the half-frozen mixture into a bowl and whisk briefly until smooth. Fold in the whisked egg white. Pour the mixture back into the container and freeze for about 6 hours.

Remove the sorbet from the freezer about 20 minutes before serving and transfer to the fridge.

M

HEALTH STATISTICS
This sorbet provides vitamin C from the pineapple and citrus juices, which helps boost immunity and protect against cancer and premature ageing.

APPLE AND APRICOT COMPOTE

MAKES 4 SERVINGS
125 G (4 OZ) DRIED ORGANIC APRICOTS (UNSULPHURED)
450 G (1 LB) APPLES, PEELED, CORED AND CHOPPED
1 TABLESPOON (15 ML) CLEAR HONEY
JUICE OF 1 LEMON
1/2–1 TEASPOON (2.5–5 ML) GROUND CINNAMON

Soak the apricots in a little hot water for at least 2 hours. Alternatively leave to soak in the fridge overnight.

Drain and chop the apricots.

Put the apples, honey, lemon juice and cinnamon in a saucepan. Add the apricots together with their soaking liquid. Stir and bring to the boil. Reduce the heat and simmer for 10 minutes until the fruit is just tender. Allow to cool.

Spoon the fruit mixture into 4 serving dishes.

Serve this compote with natural or Greek yoghurt and a drizzle of maple syrup.

HEALTH STATISTICS
Apples are rich in fibre, potassium and the flavanoid, quercetin, which has anticancer and anti-inflammatory actions. Dried apricots are rich in betacarotene and iron.

SPICED HUNZA APRICOT COMPOTE

MAKES 4 SERVINGS

250G (9 OZ) DRIED HUNZA APRICOTS

3–4 WHOLE CLOVES

3 SLICES OF FRESH GINGER, CRUSHED

2 ORANGES

1 TABLESPOON (15 ML) MAPLE SYRUP OR ACACIA HONEY

1 STICK OF CINNAMON

3–4 CARDAMOM PODS

Cover the apricots with about 500 ml (16 fl oz) hot water and leave to soak overnight.

Peel the oranges using a vegetable peeler. Divide the oranges into segments and roughly chop.

Place the orange peel, cloves, ginger, apricots and their soaking liquid in a saucepan. Add in the chopped orange, maple syrup or honey, cinnamon stick (snapped in half) and cardamom pods.

Bring to the boil and then turn down the heat to gently poach for 8–10 minutes until the apricots are softened. Allow to cool in the cooking liquid then divide into 4 individual bowls.

D

HEALTH STATISTICS
Dried apricots are rich in iron and betacarotene, a powerful antioxidant that combats premature ageing, heart disease and cancer.

RASPBERRY AND BLUEBERRY MOUSSE

MAKES 4 SERVINGS
125 G (4 OZ) BLUEBERRIES
225 G (8 OZ) RASPBERRIES
300 G (10 OZ) SILKEN TOFU
2 TABLESPOONS (30 ML) CLEAR HONEY

Reserve a few raspberries and blueberries for decoration. Place the remaining fruit in a blender or food processor with the tofu and honey. Blend until smooth. Divide into 4 individual dishes.

Decorate with the reserved fruit. Chill in the fridge and serve.

D

HEALTH STATISTICS
Blueberries are rich in phytonutrients and have the highest antioxidant capacity of all fresh fruit. Both blueberries and raspberries are rich in vitamin C. This dessert is also a good source of protein and calcium (from the tofu).

STRAWBERRY JELLY

MAKE 4 SERVINGS

**1 HEAPED TABLESPOON (15 ML) AGAR-AGAR FLAKES
(OR 1 SACHET OF POWDERED AGAR-AGAR)
200 ML (7 FL OZ) WATER
400 ML (7 FL OZ) CRANBERRY AND RASPBERRY JUICE
250 G (9 OZ) FRESH OR FROZEN STRAWBERRIES**

Mix together the agar-agar and water in a small saucepan. Bring to the boil, whisking continuously, reduce the heat and simmer for 4–5 minutes.

Add the fruit juice and mix together. Leave to cool.

Divide the strawberries between 4 glass dessert bowls and pour the cooled liquid jelly over to cover the fruit.

Chill in the fridge until set.

D

HEALTH STATISTICS
This vegetarian fresh-fruit jelly is packed with vitamin C, a powerful antioxidant and immune booster.

PINEAPPLE AND MANGO

MAKES 4 SERVINGS

1 RIPE PINEAPPLE
1 LARGE MANGO
2 LIMES
2 TEASPOONS (10 ML) CLEAR ACACIA HONEY

Peel the pineapple, cut into 1 cm (½ in) rounds then cut each round into quarters.

Slice through the mango either side of the stone. Peel, then cut the flesh into cubes.

Place the fruit in a serving bowl.

Finely grate the rind from the limes and add to the fruit. Squeeze the juice then put in a small saucepan with the acacia honey. Heat gently, stirring, just until the honey has dissolved. Allow to cool.

Pour the cooled lime juice over the fruit and toss well.

HEALTH STATISTICS
Mango is rich in betacarotene and vitamin C – both antioxidant nutrients – and pineapple also provides vitamin C.

APPLE AND RASPBERRY CRUMBLE

MAKES 4–6 SERVINGS

2 LARGE COOKING APPLES, PEELED, CORED AND SLICED

125 G (4 OZ) FRESH OR FROZEN RASPBERRIES

2 TABLESPOONS (30 ML) WATER

4 TABLESPOONS (60 ML) CLEAR HONEY

60 G (2 OZ) FLAKED ALMONDS, CRUSHED

60 G (2 OZ) OATS

25 G (1 OZ) MILLET FLAKES

25 G (1 OZ) RICE FLOUR

60 G (2 OZ) DAIRY-FREE SPREAD

Preheat the oven to 190°C/375°F/Gas mark 5.

Put the prepared apples, raspberries and water into an ovenproof dish. In a saucepan, melt 2 tablespoons (30 ml) of the honey with the water over a low heat. Pour over the fruit and mix together.

Place the flaked almonds, oats, rice flour, dairy-free spread and the remaining honey in a bowl and mix together with your fingers until you have a sticky crumb mixture. Alternatively, put in a food processor and pulse until the mixture forms fine crumbs.

Spread the oat crumble over the fruit and bake in the oven for about 25 minutes until the topping is golden. Do not overbake otherwise the topping will become too hard.

D

HEALTH STATISTICS

This dessert is rich in fibre and vitamin C (from the raspberries and apples). The almonds provide protein, calcium and heart-healthy monounsaturated oils, and the oats are rich in B-vitamins and soluble fibre which helps balance blood sugar levels.

THAI FRUIT SALAD

HALF A PINEAPPLE
HALF A HONEYDEW MELON
A QUARTER OF A WATERMELON
1 STAR FRUIT
60 G (2 OZ) COCONUT FLAKES (OR 125 G (4 OZ) FRESH COCONUT)
4 PASSION FRUITS
JUICE OF 2 LIMES

Peel the pineapple and cut into quarters. Cut out and discard the tough inner core. Cut each quarter lengthwise then slice across into chunks.

Scoop out the seeds from the honeydew melon, cut into slices, peel and slice into chunks.

Cut the watermelon into chunks, discarding skin and any seeds.

Cut the star fruit into four, and then slice finely.

In a large bowl toss together the pineapple, honeydew melon, watermelon, star fruit and coconut. Halve the passion fruits and scoop out their pulp into a separate bowl. Mix in the lime juice, then pour over the mixed fruit, and toss together. Cover and chill until serving.

D

HEALTH STATISTICS
This fruit salad is rich in vitamin C, potassium and fibre. Watermelon is also rich in lycopene, an antioxidant that helps prevent cancer of the stomach, colon and prostate.

PLUMS WITH ORANGE AND MINT

MAKES 4 SERVINGS

450 G (1 LB) PURPLE PLUMS
125 G (4 FL OZ) FRESH ORANGE JUICE
1 TABLESPOON (15 ML) CHOPPED FRESH MINT LEAVES
A LITTLE HONEY OR MAPLE SYRUP (OPTIONAL)

Halve the plums and remove the stones. Cut them into thin slices and place in a bowl.

Add the remaining ingredients and toss well.

Cover and chill in the fridge, stirring occasionally, for at least 2 hours.

HEALTH STATISTICS
Plums are a good source of fibre and have antioxidant benefits. They contain hydroxycinnamic acid, which is associated with a reduced risk of colon cancer.

FRESH FRUIT WITH HONEY, MINT AND LIME

JUICE AND ZEST OF 2 LIMES
2 TABLESPOONS (30 ML) ACACIA HONEY
2 TABLESPOONS (30 ML) CHOPPED FRESH MINT
1 CANTALOUPE MELON, HALVED AND SEEDED
350 G (12 OZ) STRAWBERRIES, HULLED AND HALVED
4 KIWI FRUIT, PEELED, CUT INTO 1/2-INCH PIECES
125 G (4 OZ) SEEDLESS GRAPES

Whisk lime juice and zest, honey and mint in large bowl to blend.

Using melon baller or spoon, scoop out cantaloupe.

Add all the fruit to the honey syrup in the bowl. Toss to combine. Let it stand for 15 minutes to allow the flavours to blend. Cover and chill until you are ready to serve.

D

HEALTH STATISTICS
Cantaloupe melon is super-rich in betacarotene, an antioxidant linked to a reduced risk of cancer and heart disease. Strawberries and lime juice are super-rich in vitamin C, another powerful antioxidant with proven health benefits.

MELON AND STRAWBERRIES

MAKES 4 SERVINGS
1 CANTALOUPE MELON
225 G (8 OZ) STRAWBERRIES
GRATED ZEST AND JUICE OF 1 LIME
150 ML (5 FL OZ) APPLE JUICE
1 TABLESPOON (15 ML) CHOPPED FRESH MINT

Remove the seeds from the melon. Cut the flesh into bite-sized pieces or scoop out with a melon baller.

Wash, hull and halve the strawberries.

Combine the prepared fruit with the lime zest and juice and apple juice in a large bowl. Just before serving, stir in the chopped fresh mint.

This dessert is delicious served on its own or with a dollop of Greek yoghurt or crème fraîche.

HEALTH STATISTICS
Cantaloupe melon is super-rich in betacarotene, and strawberries and limes are super-rich in vitamin C. Both are powerful anticancer nutrients.

INDEX